Original title: Airsoft: Tactics and Strategies

©Airsoft: Tactics and Strategies, Carlos Martínez Cerdá and Víctor Martínez Cerdá, 2025

Authors: Víctor Martínez Cerdá and Carlos Martínez Cerdá (V&C Brothers)

© Cover and illustrations: V&C Brothers

Layout and design: V&C Brothers

AIRSOFT

TACTICS AND STRATEGIES

INDEX

Chapter 1: Fundamentals of Airsoft

1.1

What is Airsoft and How Did It Originate?

Airsoft is a tactical simulation sport in which players use replica firearms that shoot small plastic pellets, known as BBs, usually 6 mm in diameter.

Unlike paintball, airsoft emphasizes realism: the replicas closely mimic the appearance, weight, and external function of real firearms, and they do not leave paint marks.

As a result, the game relies on the honesty of players to acknowledge when they've been hit.

Matches can range from quick skirmishes to elaborate military simulations known as "milsim," which can last from a few hours to several days.

The origins of airsoft trace back to Japan in the 1970s, where strict gun laws led to the development of replicas capable of firing projectiles without causing harm.

These early replicas were spring-powered and shot at low velocity.

In 1985, the Japanese company Tokyo Marui revolutionized the hobby by introducing the first automatic electric replicas, known as AEGs (Airsoft Electric Guns), allowing players to simulate automatic fire with impressive realism.

From there, the airsoft phenomenon quickly spread across Asia, especially to Taiwan and South Korea, and later made its way to Europe.

In Europe, airsoft began to gain traction in the 1990s, especially in countries such as the United Kingdom,

France, Italy, Germany, and Spain.

In the UK, for example, there are more than 4,000 registered active players and dozens of legal fields.

In France, it's estimated that there are around 10,000 regular participants, while in Germany, where the sport is heavily regulated, there are believed to be between 7,000 and 9,000 active players.

Italy also has a vibrant community, with over 8,000 enthusiasts and a growing tradition in milsim games.

Spain, for its part, has more than 15,000 players spread across local clubs and teams, with strong presence in regions such as Madrid, Catalonia, Andalusia, and Valencia.

In Europe, airsoft evolved with a strong focus on realism and military simulation.

Historical reenactment groups and military-inspired units helped shape a more structured style of play, incorporating hierarchies, radio communication, tactical maps, and complex objectives.

In addition, many associations developed common regulations to standardize power limits, minimum engagement distances, and safety rules, which allowed for the organization of international events and tournaments.

In the Americas, airsoft grew more slowly, initially overshadowed by paintball.

However, starting in the 2000s, airsoft experienced a surge in popularity, especially in the United States, where today it's estimated there are over 500,000 active players.

The realism of the replicas attracted law enforcement and military units, who adopted airsoft as a tool for tactical training.

In countries like Mexico, Argentina, Brazil, and Chile,
the sport has also been gaining followers, with estimated
numbers ranging between 5,000 and 15,000 players per
country, though often facing shifting regulations.

Globally, it's estimated that there are over 1 million active
airsoft players, with significant concentrations in the United
States, Western Europe, and East Asia.

What makes airsoft so popular is its unique combination
of strategy, adrenaline, teamwork, and realistic simulation.

It is both a sport and a form of tactical immersion and
military-style recreation.

Today, airsoft is much more than just a game: it's a global
community with events, tournaments, conventions, specialty
stores, and a culture of honor and discipline that continues
to grow worldwide.

1.2

The Difference Between Playing and Operating Strategically.

In airsoft, there is a fundamental difference between simply "playing" and truly "operating with strategy," and this distinction marks the transition from a casual participant to a committed tactical player.

Playing, in the context of airsoft, usually involves a more relaxed attitude, focused on the immediate experience of the skirmish: running, shooting, hiding, and eliminating opponents without much prior planning or in-depth analysis of the environment or objectives.

It is a valid way to enjoy the sport, but it's often limited by constant improvisation, individualistic use of the replica, and a lack of coordination with other team members.

In contrast, operating strategically means understanding that airsoft, beyond the exchange of fire, is a game of intelligence, anticipation, and teamwork.

The strategic player doesn't just ask "who can I eliminate?" but rather "how can I accomplish the objective efficiently, protect my team, and use the terrain to my advantage?"

This involves studying the field before the match, memorizing cover points, escape routes, high-risk zones, and possible enemy positions.

For example, a player operating with strategy in an urban field won't just run from building to building. Instead, they will advance while covering blind spots, coordinating with their teammate, using the echo of gunfire to detect movement, and planning entry and exit routes before every action.

A typical case can be seen in milsim games, where strategic players follow a tactical hierarchy: there is a commander, a squad leader, communication radios, and maps with assigned zones.

Every movement is calculated.

If a building needs to be captured, it is not approached head-on and hastily, but rather surrounded; suppressive fire is laid down from an elevated position, a flanking team is sent, and the right moment to enter is carefully chosen.

Here, every player has a role and understands their function within a larger operation.

They don't act on impulse, but based on tactical necessity.

The difference is also evident in how gear is used.

A player who is simply "playing" might carry equipment that looks visually appealing without considering its functionality.

In contrast, someone operating strategically selects their replica, magazines, radio, goggles, and vest based on their role and the type of game.

For example, a player acting as a sniper won't carry grenades or heavy gear: they focus on stealth, terrain-appropriate camouflage, and knowing when to move and when to remain still.

Meanwhile, a support player will be responsible for covering movement routes, holding key positions, and laying down constant fire to allow teammates to advance.

The mindset also changes.

A player without a strategy often gets frustrated easily when eliminated or if they fail to make a direct impact on the game.

The tactical operator, on the other hand, understands that their contribution can be silent yet decisive: keeping an enemy occupied, protecting the rear, relaying information over the radio, or simply holding an area can be more valuable than taking out multiple opponents.

They know when to advance, when to hold position, and, above all, when to let another player take the lead if the situation calls for it.

1.3

Safety, Legality, and Fair Play.

These are the three fundamental pillars that uphold the responsible practice of airsoft.

Although it is a sport that simulates armed combat, airsoft is neither violent nor dangerous when the basic principles of protection, respect for the law, and player ethics are followed.

Safety begins with the mandatory use of eye protection.

Airsoft BBs, although lightweight, can reach speeds between 250 and 550 FPS (feet per second), which is enough to cause injuries if they hit the eyes, mouth, or other sensitive areas.

For this reason, the use of certified ballistic goggles (ANSI Z87+ or higher) is essential in any type of game, even when preparing or testing your replica outside the playing field.

Many fields also recommend facial protection (mesh or reinforced plastic masks), especially in CQB games, where engagement distances are extremely short.

Additionally, It's crucial to wear appropriate clothing that covers arms and legs, gloves to protect fingers from hits, and sturdy footwear to reduce the risk of sprains or falls while running.

Regarding legality, this varies significantly from one country to another, and every player must be informed about the specific regulations in their region.

For example, in Spain, airsoft replicas are classified as recreational-sporting weapons, but they must be registered with the Civil Guard and are subject to power limits:

generally, 350 FPS for automatic assault replicas, 450 FPS for semi-automatic DMRs, and up to 550 FPS for manual sniper rifles.

In other countries, such as Germany, replicas with power over 0.5 joules can only fire in semi-automatic mode, and their possession is highly regulated.

In the United Kingdom, the replica must have a brightly colored section (unless the owner is registered as an active airsoft player), while in the United States, regulations vary by state, but in many cases, replicas are required to have an orange tip to distinguish them from real firearms.

Carrying a replica in public without a hard case or proper authorization can lead to detention, confiscation, or even armed intervention by law enforcement, who are not required to assume it is a toy.

Therefore, replicas must always be transported unloaded, with the battery or gas disconnected, inside a closed case, and with the ammunition stored separately.

Fair play is the soul of airsoft, since unlike paintball, where the impact leaves a visible mark, airsoft has no physical proof of a hit, so the entire system relies on the player's honesty.

If a player is hit, they must raise their hand or shout "hit!" even if no one else saw it.

Deliberately not acknowledging a hit is called "not calling the hit," and it is considered a serious breach of honor.

Those who do it repeatedly are usually expelled from fields or banned by the community.

The same applies to using illegal power levels, firing at point-blank range at prohibited areas (such as the head or genitals), shooting at referees, or ignoring minimum safety distances.

In airsoft, a player's ethics are just as important as their aim.

An example of fair play in action might be a game where a player is hit in the foot but knows no one saw it.

Even so, they stop, raise their hand, and leave the field.

That kind of behavior builds trust among players and allows the simulation to function without conflict.

The same goes for players who, when firing, refrain from emptying magazines at close range or who take on their role responsibly without cheating to gain an advantage.

Airsoft also teaches that rivalry ends on the field.

Outside the game, respect, camaraderie, and sportsmanship are expected, even between opposing teams.

Sharing advice, helping beginners, lending gear if someone forgot theirs, congratulating an opponent on a good move, or even inviting them for coffee after the match are all expressions of the community spirit that defines this sport.

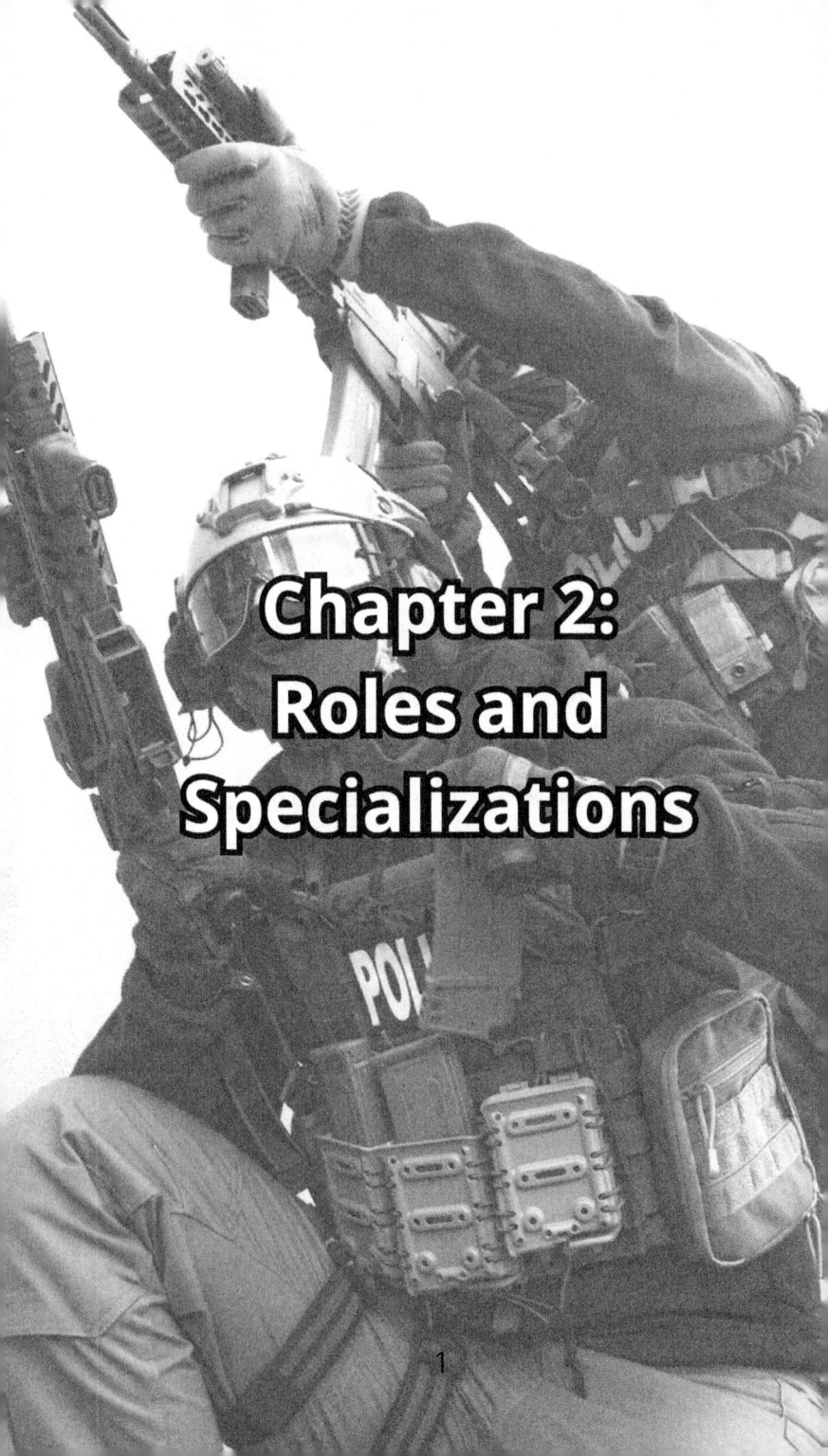

Chapter 2: Roles and Specializations

2.1

Assaulter.

In airsoft, the role of the assaulter is one of the most dynamic, active, and essential within any tactical team.

This is the player who takes part in the front line of advance, the one who engages most directly with the enemy, whether in open terrain or close-quarters combat.

Their main function is to break through defenses, flank positions, advance under enemy fire, clear rooms, and maintain constant offensive pressure.

The assaulter doesn't wait for things to happen, they make them happen.

An assaulter must be ready to move quickly across the field, switch cover in a matter of seconds, and make tactical decisions under pressure.

Their playing style is defined by mobility, controlled aggression, and the ability to adapt amidst chaos.

They are the first to advance and often the first to become a target, so they need a mix of reflexes, tactical awareness, composure, and physical endurance.

They often work in pairs or trios with other assaulters or under the command of a squad leader, forming part of a pincer movement or offensive cover.

While they can operate independently in fast-paced actions, their true strength is revealed when coordinating with a team.

The assaulter's gear is usually light, functional, and efficient.

They use electric assault replicas (AEGs) such as M4s, G36s, AK74s, SCARs, among many others, typically configured with mid-length or short barrels for better maneuverability.

They usually carry between 3 and 6 magazines on their vest, a secondary weapon (such as a GBB or AEP pistol), and often a sound, smoke, or BB grenade for quick assaults in confined spaces.

It's also common for them to wear padded protection on knees and elbows to dive to the ground or crawl without injury, as well as tactical gloves, ballistic goggles, and a lightweight helmet or beret depending on the game's setting.

The assaulter's mindset is very specific: they must be ready to dive into danger without hesitation, but also know when to stop and fall back.

It's not about charging in recklessly like a kamikaze, but rather seizing the exact tactical moment to strike hard.

For example, when their team is firing from a position and the enemy is focused elsewhere, the assaulter can flank from the side, move silently within a few meters of the enemy, and attack from an unexpected angle.

Their success depends on speed, boldness, and calculated timing.

In CQB games (close-quarter environments like buildings, factories, or urban towns), the assaulter is vital.

They're the first to enter a room, the one who clears corners quickly, and the one who secures hallways so the rest of the team can advance.

They must know how to move in a zigzag pattern, how to use shadows to their advantage, how to peek without exposing their whole body, and how to throw a grenade and enter in sync.

A poorly coordinated action in CQB can result in the entire team's elimination, so verbal communication or hand signals is essential.

In open field games, their role shifts slightly: they advance between trees, mounds, or structures, always seeking cover and observing flanking routes.

In this setting, the assaulter must learn to read the terrain: know which areas are passable, which vegetation provides concealment, and how to move without making noise.

They also need good physical conditioning, as they may have to cover hundreds of meters under the sun with full gear.

A skilled assaulter must also master the timing of fire and movement.

This means knowing when to advance while a teammate covers, and when to stop and provide cover for the next.

This technique, known as fire and movement, is the foundation of all tactical offense.

If an assaulter runs without support, they become exposed; if they wait too long, they lose the momentum of the attack.

The key lies in coordination, reflexes, and quick decision-making.

2.2

Heavy Support.

The heavy support role in airsoft is one of the most strategic and least understood, but absolutely crucial when it comes to maintaining control of the battlefield.

A heavy support operator is not simply someone who shoots a lot; they are the defensive and offensive anchor of a squad, responsible for suppressing the enemy, cutting off routes of advance, locking down enemy positions, and covering the movement of teammates.

Their job is to apply constant pressure through a high volume of fire, not necessarily to eliminate, but to keep the enemy from lifting their heads or moving freely.

Unlike the assaulter, who moves constantly, the heavy support tends to operate from a fixed or semi-static position.

Their main function is to provide covering fire: they shoot not for precision, but to deny parts of the map to the enemy, blocking windows, alleys, doors, or paths they might use to advance.

This allows teammates to flank, advance, or retreat without being hit.

In well-organized games, the support is the one who sets the pace of the engagement.

When they fire, others move; when they reload, everyone protects them.

Their gear is very distinctive and typically based on replicas of light or medium machine guns, such as the M249, M60, PKM,

RPK, Stoner LMG, or even modified versions of M4 or AK rifles equipped with drum magazines and heavy barrels.

These replicas usually have a higher rate of fire and a larger ammo capacity (ranging from 1,200 to 5,000 BBs in automatic magazines).

Generally, a support gunner does not need pinpoint accuracy: their advantage lies in volume, not precision.

However, an experienced operator can use controlled bursts to maintain tactical presence and avoid wasting ammunition unnecessarily.

The heavy support player must have a strong sense of terrain and a panoramic view of the battle.

They must identify chokepoints where the enemy is likely to pass and anticipate by setting up their position before the firefight begins.

In a woodland game, for example, the support gunner might position themselves on a hill or behind a wide log that offers cover while dominating a trail with their machine gun.

Each time movement is detected, they fire long bursts that force the enemy to take cover or retreat.

Meanwhile, their squad advances on the flanks.

In an urban scenario, they might take position in a window or at a corner with a clear view of the central courtyard, keeping the enemy pinned and unable to cross.

Support gunners also carry a greater physical load.

They usually operate with a heavier replica (between 5 and 9 kg), multiple BB bags, spare batteries, or even gas canisters if their machine gun is GBB.

For this reason, the player must have a certain level of physical endurance and know how to move efficiently without exhausting themselves.

They don't need to run as much as an assaulter, but they must be able to reposition quickly if the front shifts.

The weight of the gear also affects how they shoot: they typically fire while resting the weapon on a bipod, a backpack, or directly on the ground, using a mount or stable surface to steady the replica.

A support gunner cannot operate alone.

They always need a squad to cover them, protect them while reloading, and know how to capitalize on their suppressive fire.

If the team doesn't act accordingly, the support's effort becomes useless.

That's why in well-trained formations, there's clear synchronization: while the support lays down fire and keeps up pressure, two assaulters flank the enemy position and a third watches the rear.

There might even be a radio operator or a squad leader giving instructions on where to fire or when to reposition.

In milsim scenarios, the heavy support role is a very valuable chess piece.

An effective support operator must have discipline.

It's not about firing all the time, but about choosing the right moments: when the enemy begins to move, during a retreat, or when their team needs a distraction.

They must also know how to manage their ammunition.

Even with thousands of BBs, reloading a machine gun can take a long time, and doing it at the wrong moment can leave the entire team exposed.

A good support gunner never shoots just for the sake of shooting; they know how many magazines they have left, how many BBs are in the hopper, and which sectors need to be protected as a priority.

2.3

Designated Marksman (DMR).

The designated marksman, or DMR (Designated Marksman Rifleman), plays an intermediate role between an assault player and a sniper, both in terms of range and gameplay rhythm.

Their main function is to deliver accurate fire at medium to long distances, acting as a sort of semi-automatic sniper within the squad, but with more tactical integration and a higher rate of fire than a traditional sniper.

Unlike the sniper, who often operates entirely independently, the designated marksman works within the team, accompanying the main unit or acting from advanced support positions, making a difference in mid-range engagements where precision is critical.

The DMR is trained to detect, identify, and neutralize strategic targets such as other marksmen, squad leaders, enemy support gunners, or enemy snipers.

They also have the capability to provide long-range cover in urban or open-field combat, especially in situations where assault rifles can't accurately hit the target.

For example, in a woodland setting, when a squad is advancing and comes under fire from a hill 70 meters away, the DMR can move to a lateral position and eliminate the enemy shooters with just a few well-placed shots.

They don't need to advance constantly, but must know when to reposition and when to hold their ground.

In terms of gear, the DMR uses specific replicas of semi-automatic precision rifles, modified to shoot at longer ranges and with greater stability than a standard assault rifle.

The most common replicas for this role include variants like the SR-25, M14 EBR, SCAR-H, AR-10, or even modernized G3 rifles, all configured to fire in semi-automatic mode.

These replicas are usually internally upgraded with precision barrels, tuned hop-up chambers, stronger springs, and electronic trigger systems (MOSFETs) to improve responsiveness.

In most fields, DMRs are allowed higher power limits than standard AEGs, typically between 400 and 450 FPS, but are restricted to semi-automatic fire and must respect minimum engagement distances (for example, not firing under 15 or 20 meters).

The player who takes on this role must have accurate aim, strong breath control, good trigger discipline, and above all, strong tactical awareness.

They often need to stay calm while the rest of the team moves and choose their targets wisely.

They don't shoot at just anyone; they pick high-value targets.

For example, if an enemy squad is advancing, the DMR might focus on eliminating the support gunner or the squad leader, creating confusion and disruption.

They can also lock down a long corridor from a window or cover a road from a second story, forcing the enemy to find alternate routes.

Although not a pure sniper, the DMR must also master camouflage and concealment skills, especially when operating alone or from elevated positions.

They must know how to blend into their surroundings, how to move without being detected, and how to identify threats before those threats spot them.

They must also be proficient with optics: a medium magnification scope (from 3x to 6x) is ideal for this type of engagement, allowing them to observe without needing to get too close, and to shoot accurately without relying on automatic fire.

A concrete example of how a DMR operates can be seen in milsim-style games.

Let's say a squad needs to move through a narrow forest path and suspects an ambush ahead.

The DMR moves ahead discreetly, climbs onto a rock or hides in a spot with good visibility, and scans the path using their optics.

They detect movement, identify a fortified position, and take out the lookout with a clean shot.

They then report over the radio to the squad leader, who can decide to change routes or proceed with covering fire.

In that scenario, the DMR wasn't just a shooter, they were the squad's forward eyes, the human sensor who detected the threat in advance.

2.4

Sniper.

The sniper role is probably one of the most attractive and cinematic, but also one of the most complex, demanding, and solitary.

It's not just about having a long-range replica and shooting from afar.

The sniper is a specialist in patience, precision, camouflage, and terrain analysis, acting as an advanced observer, neutralizer of strategic threats, and real-time intelligence gatherer for their team.

Their goal is not to rack up kills, but to destabilize the enemy from a distance, cut off their lines of advance, and sow doubt in what they consider a safe zone.

The sniper's primary replica is usually a manual bolt-action rifle, specially modified to reach distances beyond those of a standard AEG.

Models like the VSR-10, L96, M40, or variants of the SSG24 are among the most popular.

These rifles are equipped with high-power springs, precision barrels ranging from 500 to 650 mm, finely adjustable hop-up units, and reinforced internal systems.

In most fields, these replicas can reach up to 550 FPS, but they must always follow mandatory minimum engagement distances (for example, no shooting under 25 or 30 meters), and bolt action is often required so the player doesn't have a high rate of fire.

This rifle is paired with a secondary replica, usually a pistol or a compact submachine gun, for personal defense in case of close-quarters combat.

But a sniper's success does not rely solely on the weapon, it lies in their ability to move silently, read the environment, use active camouflage, and maintain constant observation.

A good sniper doesn't move just for the sake of it; they glide with the calm precision of a predator.

They know how to crawl through branches without snapping them, how to conceal their silhouette with natural vegetation or a ghillie suit, how to blend into a shadow and become invisible, even just meters from the enemy.

A real example of this is when a sniper hides for twenty minutes without moving behind a dry bush in a woodland game, and at the precise moment, eliminates an enemy radio operator about to call for reinforcements, thus changing the course of the game.

The sniper also acts as an advanced sensor for the team.

Although often operating alone or in a duo with a spotter, their role goes beyond shooting: they detect enemy positions, patrol routes, tactical movements, and can even mark targets for the team using signals or radio communication.

In a milsim game, the sniper becomes a vital reconnaissance tool.

They can infiltrate behind enemy lines, observe the behavior of a rival base for half an hour, and then return with critical information about weak points, supply routes, or surveillance patterns.

The shot itself is only the final step in a long sequence.

A good sniper spends more time waiting than shooting.

They make no noise, give away no clues, and only pull the trigger when they know they can eliminate the target and vanish.

If the shot misses, their position is compromised, and they become a top-priority target.

That's why, beyond precision, a sniper needs a planned escape route, must know how to move to a secondary position without being detected, and have the discipline not to shoot, even with a clear target, if it jeopardizes the mission.

Camouflage is an art.

The best snipers don't use off-the-shelf ghillie suits; they customize them by hand, adding local vegetation, applying paint, cutting nets, and even deliberately dirtying their gear to reduce shine.

They adjust their silhouette so it doesn't resemble the human form.

They know that any visible part—the scope lens, an ungloved finger, a bit of wrist—can give them away.

And if they're discovered, they know how to stay perfectly still, control their breathing, and wait for the enemy to pass by, as if they were part of the environment.

Psychologically, the sniper role is demanding.

It requires solitude, self-control, constant self-correction, and a high tolerance for frustration.

It's common to go long periods without taking a single shot, yet under high tension.

There are games in which a sniper may stay infiltrated for an hour and fire only one shot, but that single shot might take out the enemy squad leader just before an offensive, completely shifting the balance of the match.

A sniper can't be someone who improvises.

The role requires specific training: understanding BB drop at various distances, adjusting the hop-up based on temperature, knowing how to read the wind, correcting shots after the first impact, and managing the fear of being discovered.

For this reason, in many squads, the sniper role is assigned only to players with experience, discipline, and a strong commitment to simulation.

Chapter 3:
Training and
Teamwork

3.1

Principles of Squad Work.

The principles of squad work make the difference between a group of players simply wearing the same uniform and a tactically cohesive team capable of operating as a real unit.

The squad is the basic organizational cell in any tactical group, and its effectiveness is based on constant communication, mutual trust, role specialization, fire and movement discipline, and the pursuit of shared objectives.

Each member has a function that not only defines their play style but also their responsibility within the overall mechanism, as this is not about individual performances, but a single body operating with multiple coordinated limbs.

A squad in airsoft typically consists of between 4 and 8 players, though this can vary depending on the event or mission.

Ideally, each member should have a clear role: squad leader, assault troopers, heavy support, designated marksman...

This division is not decorative, it determines how the unit moves, how it reacts to threats, and how it executes an assault, a defense, or a retreat.

For example, if the leader orders an assault on an occupied building, the assault troopers advance first along the flanks, the support lays down constant covering fire from a secure position, and the DMR takes out lookouts in elevated windows.

All of this happens within seconds, but it only works if each member knows what to do without having to ask.

Communication is vital.

Having radios isn't enough, you need clear protocols.

Short phrases, established codes, key names for areas of the map or specific roles.

A good squad doesn't shout over each other; they understand each other with minimal words.

For example, if someone says "two contacts, direction three, behind cover," the rest already knows there are two enemies to the right, they're protected, and they can adjust their positions accordingly.

If the leader says "Red, flank; Blue, covering fire," the teams act without hesitation.

This fluidity isn't improvised, it's trained.

An efficient squad practices synchronized movements, hand signals, rotating roles, and fire-and-movement drills.

Trust is also a fundamental pillar.

Each player must be able to rely on their teammate to cover their advance, follow the strategy, and not compromise the team's position.

That's why squad work also means respecting the group's pace, even if one feels they could move faster.

If a player breaks formation to charge alone at the enemy, they can put the rest at risk and destabilize the structure.

On the other hand, if everyone acts within the plan, even a small squad can hold off larger forces.

A clear example occurs in an urban match:

four well-coordinated players, covering 360°, with overlapping fields of fire and constant communication, can defend an entire street without needing reinforcements, as long as they stick together.

The principle of fire and movement is another foundation of squad work.

While some players fire to keep the enemy pinned down, others move.

This technique allows for advancement without exposure.

It requires precise timing when providing cover, choosing the right moment to move, and always keeping angles covered.

Not everyone fires at the same time, they take turns to ensure there's never a moment of silence the enemy can exploit.

This mechanic is first trained in pairs, then trios, and finally with the full squad.

Another key principle is objective discipline.

A well-trained squad doesn't scatter or chase personal eliminations.

If the mission is to capture a point, secure a building, or escort a VIP, that objective takes priority over any engagement.

This requires emotional control and focus.

If an enemy appears but does not pose a direct threat, the correct decision might be to ignore them so as not to compromise the mission.

These kinds of decisions are what transform a group of players into a true tactical team.

A well-executed example of squad work can be seen in a simulated rescue mission.

The squad is divided into two teams: Alpha and Bravo.

Alpha advances on the right, laying down covering fire and clearing rooms.

Bravo moves silently on the left, looking for access to the building where the hostage is located.

The DMR in the rear marks potential threats.

The heavy support sets up in a key position to cover the retreat.

When Bravo extracts the hostage, Alpha covers the withdrawal and the support lays down smoke to block enemy vision.

None of this happens by chance, it's because the squad has practiced similar scenarios and each player knows their role.

In short, squad work in airsoft is not simply being together on the field, it's thinking as a unit, moving as a unit, and acting as a unit.

It's understanding that victory doesn't depend on who shoots the most, but on who coordinates best.

A well-trained squad can dominate the field without needing numerical superiority.

Its strength lies in the precision of its movements, the clarity of its decisions, and the strength of its internal bonds.

When this happens, airsoft ceases to be just a shooting game and becomes a true tactical experience, where every member matters and every action has a purpose.

3.2

Tactical Communication:
Signals, Codes, and Radios.

Tactical communication in airsoft is one of the most decisive elements for a squad's success on the field.

It doesn't matter how accurate a player is or how advanced their gear may be, if they can't transmit information clearly, quickly, and securely, their effectiveness is drastically reduced.

Tactical communication is not just about talking: it's about coordinating movements, anticipating threats, alerting teammates to enemy positions, and delivering orders without creating confusion.

This is achieved through three fundamental tools: hand signals, verbal codes, and efficient use of radios.

Hand signals are the silent language of airsoft.

In scenarios where stealth is crucial, speaking can give away the team's position.

That's why every trained squad develops and practices a standardized set of gestures to communicate essential orders or information without making a sound.

For example, a raised hand might mean "stop," two fingers in a V shape pointing to the eyes can indicate "enemy in sight," a closed fist may mean "hold" or "get ready."

Pointing with two fingers to the right or left can signal "flank clear" or "move in that direction."

During a room entry, the lead operator can use one hand to indicate how many enemies are inside, while using the other to signal a countdown for the breach.

These signals must be clear, visible, and repeated through training until every player understands them instinctively.

It's not about inventing gestures in each game, but rather using a shared language, just like a real military team would.

Verbal codes, on the other hand, allow players to communicate specific information in real time when speaking doesn't compromise the mission.

This doesn't mean speaking freely, but rather using short phrases, numerical codes, or designated names for locations, objectives, and roles.

For example, instead of saying "I'm going to that house on the left with two windows and a red door," a trained player will say "moving to Alpha 2," if that structure has already been designated as such during the team briefing.

Likewise, "two contacts, Bravo 3, direction 11" might mean there are two enemies in the area designated Bravo 3, approaching from the right.

Common codes also include terms like "negative" (no), "affirmative" (yes), "clear" (no enemies), "contaminated" (area with enemies), "over" (pass of communication over radio), and "out" (end of transmission).

When used properly, these terms prevent misunderstandings and speed up decision-making.

A real example: during a game in a forested area, a squad leader hears on the radio, "multiple contacts, Charlie 1, direction 9, need support," and can immediately send a team to intercept or cover the zone, without wasting time on further explanation.

Radios are the backbone of long-distance tactical communication.

It's common for entire squads to use short-range radios (such as PMR446), equipped with headsets and PTT (push-to-talk) buttons mounted on the chest or weapon.

Proper radio use doesn't mean constant chatter, but knowing when, how, and what to say.

Irresponsible use of the channel can clog it and block critical messages, which is why well-organized teams assign specific frequencies to each squad, and only the squad leader or designated radio operator communicates with central command.

Within the squad, messages must be concise: "Echo 1, taking cover position," "Sniper spotted, tall building in Delta 4," "Support ready, awaiting fire order."

Using "over" and "out" helps indicate whether the channel is in use or free, and prevents players from speaking over one another.

Some advanced squads even use encrypted codes or key phrases for sensitive situations, for example, "package secure" to refer to a rescued hostage, or "crow in the nest" to indicate a sniper is in position.

The combination of these three systems—hand signals, verbal codes, and radios—allows for smooth coordination even in the most chaotic environments.

In a practical example, a squad approaching a building may advance silently to within 10 meters of the entrance.

The squad leader then gives a hand signal to stop,

followed by holding up three fingers to indicate a countdown.

Another operator, already in cover, communicates over the radio: "Interior clear from my angle, no visuals in upper windows, over."

The leader responds: "Alpha breaching in three, two, one, out."

And the operation is carried out with a level of synchronization that can only be achieved through practice.

3.3

Coordination and Synchronization of Movements.

Coordination and synchronization of movement are the essence of any successful tactical operation.

No matter how skilled an individual player may be, if their team doesn't move as a single unit, any strategy will fall apart against a more organized enemy.

Coordinating movements isn't simply about walking together or following in a line.

It means knowing who advances and who provides cover, when to move, in which direction, and at what pace, all under a shared objective and with the ability to adapt to unforeseen events without falling into chaos.

Tactical synchronization allows the execution of complex maneuvers such as flanking, fire-and-move advances, building assaults, crossfire defenses, and ambushes with a level of precision that maximizes collective impact.

A team that masters coordination moves with purpose.

If a pair advances on the left flank, the team on the right doesn't move at the same time, they provide covering fire or visual support.

When the first pair reaches a cover point, they signal the others to move.

This is the classic principle of "fire and movement," where one element provides cover while the other advances, allowing progress without becoming completely exposed.

If both groups were to move at the same time, a well-placed enemy burst would be enough to neutralize the entire squad.

Synchronization here is not just visual or intuitive, it must be trained.

Over time, players learn to trust each other's movements, to anticipate their actions, and to respond without the need for explicit commands.

A clear example occurs in urban scenarios.

Let's suppose a squad needs to enter a narrow street where enemy presence is suspected; in this case, not everyone rushes in at once.

The heavy support positions itself first at a corner and covers the field with its machine gun.

Then, the assault members cross one by one, covered by that potential fire, and take position on the opposite facade.

Once two players are in the forward position, they give the all-clear and the rest of the team follows.

This action may seem simple, but if someone moves ahead before the support is ready, or if one of the assaulters runs before the previous one has covered, the entire maneuver collapses.

Synchronization also applies when entering buildings.

In a CQB-style assault, operators do not enter chaotically: each one has an assigned sector.

The first covers the immediate right angle, the second the left, the third the front, and the fourth stays in reserve or covers a secondary door.

They all enter one after another with a fraction of a second between them, in a rehearsed, fast, and almost choreographed sequence.

If one of them stops, hesitates, or enters too early, fields of fire overlap, and the risk of friendly fire or casualties increases.

This synchronization is practiced dry many times before being executed in the field, using simulated spaces and repeated movements until they become instinctive.

Another key aspect is rhythm management, as it's not always about advancing quickly.

Sometimes coordination means knowing when to pause, wait for a lagging teammate, regroup, or halt the advance to allow the DMR or sniper to neutralize a threat before proceeding.

A coordinated squad doesn't accelerate for the sake of speed: it adapts its pace to the slowest member when the situation requires it and maintains order even in moments of stress.

This results in a visual image of discipline on the field: players moving in lines, not crowding each other, entering spaces one by one, turning to cover different angles, and positioning themselves without getting in each other's way.

Coordination also extends to more complex maneuvers, such as double-pincer flanks.

In this case, while one group keeps the enemy occupied from the front, another circles around from one side, and a third infiltrates from the rear.

This operation only works if all three groups are synchronized.

If the flanking group moves ahead before those at the front have opened fire, they risk being detected and neutralized.

If those meant to distract the enemy act too late, the enemy may move or retreat.

Everything depends on near-millimetric tactical timing, based on signals, practice, and knowledge of the team's behavior.

Even in defense, coordination is vital.

A team defending a structure must divide responsibilities: who watches each entrance, who covers the windows, who is ready to move if a teammate goes down, and who has access to extra ammunition or medical supplies.

When an attacker breaches, there's no time to decide, each player knows their role and acts without asking.

3.4

Leadership on the Field.

Leadership on the airsoft field is one of the most difficult qualities to develop and, at the same time, one of the most decisive in determining the outcome of any operation.

It's not simply about giving orders or assuming a position of authority, but about guiding, organizing, anticipating, and maintaining group cohesion amid the chaos of simulated combat.

A good squad leader is not necessarily the most experienced player or the one who shoots the most, but the one who can read the terrain, stay calm under pressure, make clear decisions at critical moments, and, above all, inspire confidence in their team.

In airsoft, where communication, tactics, and adaptation are constant, the leader is the one who translates the pre-game plan into concrete actions on the ground.

They are the one who sets the routes of advance, distributes roles, assigns watch sectors, and decides when to move, when to defend, and when to attack.

Their voice, whether literal or symbolic, is what holds the group together.

And the moment that voice goes silent—because it hesitates, falters, or fails to convey confidence—the squad begins to fall apart.

That's why leadership is not just a technical skill, but a deeply emotional one.

A good squad leader in airsoft is someone who listens before speaking, who knows their teammates' strengths and weaknesses, and positions them based on their actual skills, not on hierarchy.

If they know one of their players is an excellent marksman but nervous under pressure, they'll assign them to a watch or rear guard position.

If they have an aggressive and fast player, they'll use them as the spearhead.

The leader adapts the strategy to the team they have, not to the ideal they imagine.

In the middle of the game, the leader must be the cool head.

If the enemy attacks from an unexpected flank and a teammate panics, the leader doesn't yell or get frustrated.

They reorganize, give a clear order, reposition.

For example, if a squad is advancing along a narrow path and suddenly comes under crossfire from a hill, the leader doesn't allow everyone to return fire chaotically.

They order: "Echo covers right, Bravo falls back 15 meters and flanks left, Alpha lays down suppressive fire," and in seconds they've turned an ambush into a defensive maneuver that can shift into an offensive if executed quickly.

Leadership also shows itself before and after combat.

In the briefing, the leader is the one who analyzes the map, interprets the mission, assigns radio frequencies, and sets extraction points and lines of advance.

He doesn't impose, he consults.

He involves the team in the planning so that every player feels the weight of the mission and acts with responsibility.

During combat, he ensures communication stays active.

He doesn't need to speak constantly, but he must know what each unit is doing.

And at the end, he is the first to take responsibility for mistakes, to give recognition, and to assess what happened in order to improve in the next match.

Another key aspect of leadership in airsoft is managing the emotional rhythm of the team.

There are long games, intense scenarios, difficult conditions.

The leader is the one who senses fatigue, discouragement, or confusion.

He knows when to call a break, when to reorganize, when to lift spirits with a timely phrase.

If the team has suffered several consecutive losses or a tactical defeat, the leader doesn't look for blame, he looks for solutions.

"We lost structure in the second phase, let's regroup, reorganize, and go out again with a clear head."

That attitude is contagious and lifts the team.

Leadership also means giving up individual spotlight.

Many times, the leader is the one who shoots the least, because he is focused on observing, deciding, and communicating.

He doesn't run across the field chasing eliminations,

but moves with caution, maintaining visibility over the whole team and the ability to react.

In some cases, the leader doesn't even participate directly on the front line.

He stays in the rear with a radio, coordinating three squads from an elevated position, like a true tactical commander.

Other times, he leads from the front, setting the example during a risky advance, knowing that his team's morale rises when they see him move forward without hesitation.

There are also moments when leadership must be shared.

A good leader knows when to delegate.

If the team splits into two groups, he appoints a second-in-command.

If he is eliminated in combat, there's already a protocol in place for someone else to take command so the unit isn't left directionless.

This foresight is a sign of mature leadership: knowing that the objective is more important than the ego of the one in charge.

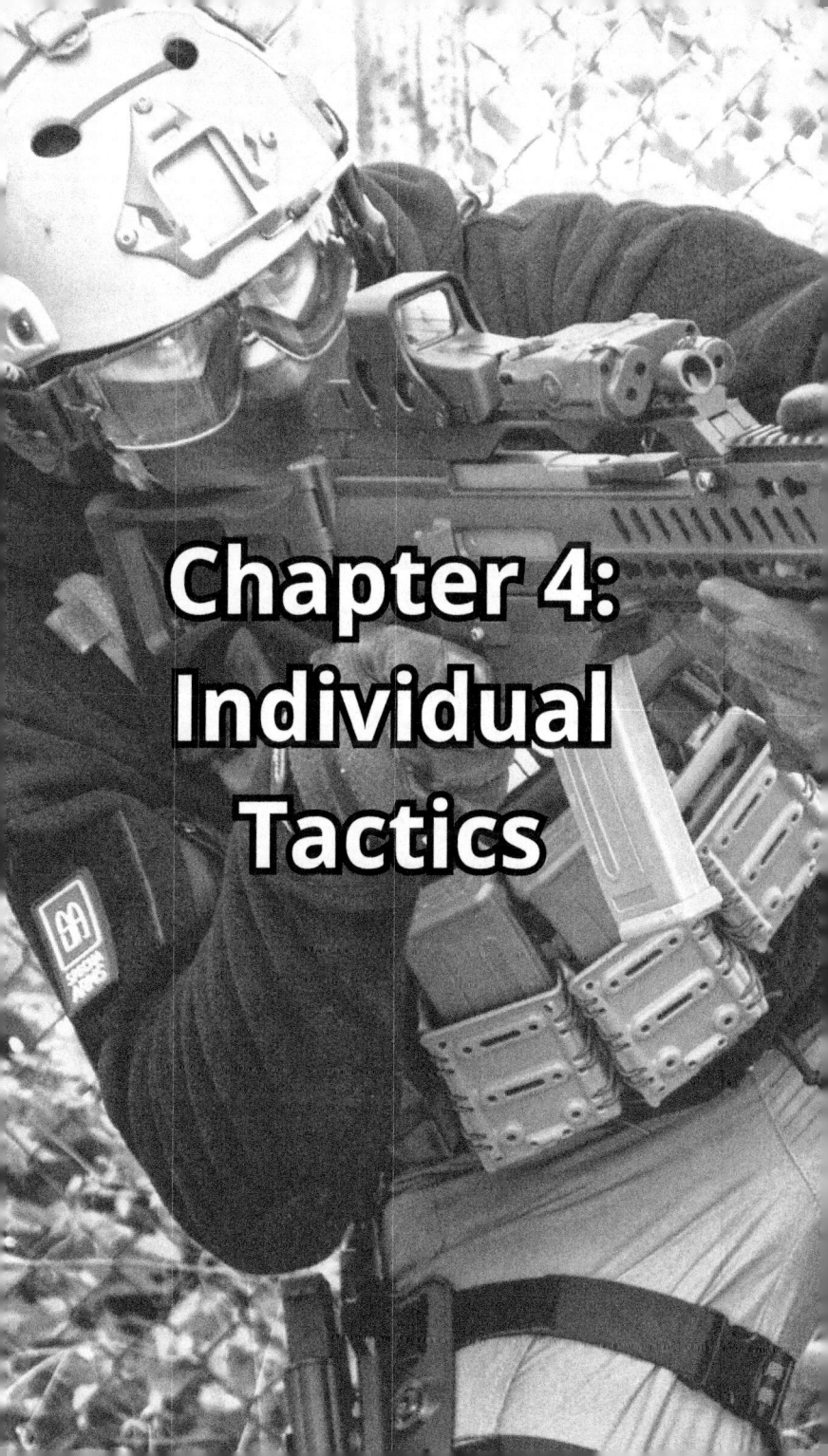

Chapter 4: Individual Tactics

4.1

Tactical Movement:
Advancing Without Becoming a Target.

Tactical movement is one of the most important skills a player can develop, and one of the least practiced by those who focus only on shooting.

Knowing how to advance without becoming a target is not just about crouching while running or moving from cover to cover. It involves applying a series of principles that combine stealth, terrain awareness, intelligent use of the environment, situational awareness, and teamwork.

To move tactically means to move with intent, calculation, and control, minimizing exposure while increasing the chances of survival and success.

The first principle is understanding that the human body has a recognizable silhouette.

When a player moves in a straight line, upright, in open terrain, their figure stands out easily against any background.

On the other hand, when crouching, moving in a zigzag pattern, or using shadows, vegetation, walls, or elevation changes, their silhouette breaks up, blends with the environment, and becomes much harder to identify.

This is why one of the most common mistakes made by beginners is to advance in a straight line at full speed toward cover, creating noise, agitation, and being spotted from afar.

A trained player, by contrast, takes time to observe first, calculate the distance, and move only when they know exactly where their next cover point will be.

The use of cover is essential, but not every object qualifies as useful cover.

It's important to distinguish between real cover (which stops BBs) and concealment (which only blocks the line of sight).

A bush might hide you, but it won't protect you if the enemy has already spotted you.

A thick log or a wall, on the other hand, will.

The basic rule is always to move from cover to cover, without crossing more open space than absolutely necessary, and remaining exposed for the shortest possible time.

For example, if a player needs to cross an open yard with three trees and a wall at the far end, they won't run in a straight line, they'll move from tree to tree, taking brief pauses, and only complete the final sprint when they're certain the enemy isn't watching.

The pace of movement is also crucial.

It's not always about moving fast; sometimes, stealth is more effective than speed.

A player can advance 10 meters crouched, silently, and remain undetected, while another who runs makes noise, gives away their position, and gets eliminated.

There are moments when staying still is the best option, waiting for the enemy to reveal their position, or even falling back a few meters to take a different route.

In a real match, a player might notice that the right flank is heavily guarded.

Instead of pushing forward, they fall back 50 meters, loop around a hedge, and come in from a blind angle, eliminating two enemies who thought they were safe.

That kind of decision can only be made if the player is aware of their surroundings, observes more than they shoot, and thinks through each step before taking it.

Teamwork enhances tactical movement.

A lone player can advance, but a well-coordinated pair can cover each other and move forward without exposing themselves.

This technique is called "fire and movement," and it's one of the foundations of tactical combat.

While one advances, the other provides cover, and then they switch roles.

This can be done between two players or even with groups of four or five, where one lays down suppressive fire, another repositions, and so on until the maneuver is complete.

This type of advance not only reduces the risk of being hit but also disorients the enemy, who doesn't know who to shoot at and ends up losing ground.

In urban scenarios, this becomes even more evident: two players cover the street while the other two cross to the opposite facade, then the process is repeated to keep advancing building by building.

Terrain reading is another key factor, as a player who moves without observing the field is essentially playing blind.

On the other hand, a player who scans the area, identifies high points, shadows, passage zones, and possible enemy routes can plan their movement like a chess player moving pieces with logic.

If the terrain is uneven, they will look to move through

depressions, trenches, or behind natural elevations.

If it's a wooded field, they'll advance through areas with denser vegetation, taking care not to step on dry branches.

If it's an urban environment, they'll move close to the walls, keeping a low profile and checking angles before peeking out.

The body must also move with control.

The way the replica is held, the way the ground is stepped on, how the vest is adjusted, or how the gear is carried can make a big difference.

A player who carries their replica in a low-ready position, ready to raise and fire, is more effective than one who lets it hang and has to lift it from the waist.

The player who has adjusted their backpack and vest to avoid noise with every step will infiltrate more effectively than one walking with loose BBs, poorly sealed Velcro, or metallic keys jingling with every move.

4.2

Cover and Effective Movement.

Proper use of cover and effective movement are absolutely essential elements for surviving, holding key positions, and advancing on the field without becoming an easy target.

It doesn't matter how much your replica costs or how many BBs you can fire per minute, if you don't know how to move between cover or how to use it properly, you'll be eliminated in seconds by a more tactical and disciplined enemy.

Cover refers to any physical element in the environment that protects the player from enemy fire, not just conceals them.

Here, there is a vital distinction between "concealment" and "cover": concealment is something that prevents you from being seen (like a bush, a shadow, or a tarp), while cover is something that actually stops projectiles, such as a wall, a vehicle, a thick tree, or a trench.

Many players make the mistake of hiding behind elements that don't stop BBs, thinking they're safe when in fact they're completely exposed.

For example, a dense hedge might hide your silhouette, but if the enemy already knows your location, it won't stop them from hitting you.

On the other hand, a concrete corner, an iron pillar, or a stack of thick tires can stop multiple shots, even from crossfire angles.

Body positioning behind cover is just as important.

It's not enough to simply be "behind" something, you have to use it intelligently.

Exposing half your body to shoot, always peeking from the same side, or shooting while standing when you could shoot from a crouched position are basic mistakes that come at a high cost.

A well-trained player uses the technique of peeking from the side with the smallest possible profile, keeping their replica close to the edge and exposing only the optic, the barrel, and one eye.

This is called a "peek" and should be done briefly, like a flash: peek out, fire one or two shots, and immediately pull back.

You should never expose your body in a predictable way or for too long, as the enemy will adjust their aim and fire at the exact point where they know you'll reappear.

Another essential point is to vary your angle of exposure.

If you always shoot from the right side of cover, the enemy will know where to expect you, but if you switch sides, change levels (from standing to crouching or prone), or even fall back and find another shooting position, you'll confuse your opponent.

In a defensive situation, a player who constantly changes cover keeps their opponent guessing.

For example, if you're behind a wall with three windows, you can peek from the first, fire two shots, crouch, switch to the second, shoot again, and move to the third.

This way, even if your position is known, your point of exposure keeps changing, and that gives you an advantage.

Movements between cover must be fast, deliberate, and pre-planned.

A common mistake is running without having identified the next cover point, ending up trapped midway.

Before moving, a player should visually mark the next piece of cover, estimate the distance, and time the movement, ideally when the enemy is distracted, reloading, or under suppressive fire.

Sometimes, it's necessary to wait 20 or 30 seconds for the perfect opportunity.

For example, if a support player on your team is firing at an enemy position, that's your moment to sprint 10 meters across open ground to an abandoned vehicle you'll use as your next firing position.

If you do it without covering fire, you likely won't make it.

That's why straight-line movement in open terrain should be avoided.

Whenever possible, it's recommended to advance in a zigzag pattern, vary your height (from crouching to upright or vice versa), and make brief pauses at intermediate points to regain control of the situation.

For instance, if a player needs to reach a house at the end of a yard, they can run from one tree to another, then crouch behind a stack of pallets, assess the enemy's position, and then complete the final stretch to the house.

Each phase of movement should be a purposeful action, not a reflex.

In urban combat (CQB), cover changes: it consists of doors, pillars, overturned tables, and hallway corners.

Here, space is more limited, and every millimeter counts.

Peeking around a corner without first doing a "foot peek" (a slight lean to provoke an enemy reaction), or advancing down a hallway without a teammate covering your back, can be fatal.

In these situations, movements are shorter but also more frequent, and players often advance close to walls, always turning with their weapon raised, covering every blind angle as if expecting someone to be aiming at them.

In open fields, natural cover is equally valuable if understood correctly.

A ditch, a rock, a fallen log, or even a small rise in the terrain can provide a huge tactical advantage.

A player who knows how to read the terrain uses it to their benefit.

For example, if a hill blocks the enemy's line of sight, you can move "invisibly" to them until you're close enough to flank.

If the field has tall vegetation, you can crouch and move through it undetected, appearing unexpectedly from the flank.

Finally, efficiency in cover and movement also includes teamwork, as advancing in pairs, where one provides cover while the other moves, is a basic but extremely effective technique.

To this, you must add communication: a simple "covering" or "cross" can save your teammate from an unnecessary elimination.

The synchronization between cover and movement is what allows you to advance in situations dominated by the enemy and turn pressure into an advantage.

Mastering cover and effective movement is not a luxury,

it's a necessity for any player who wants to excel in airsoft.

It's not about moving a lot, but about moving well, with tactical purpose, using the environment as an ally and minimizing every unnecessary exposure.

On the field, the one who survives and dominates is not the fastest shooter, but the one who exposes themselves the least and moves with intelligence.

4.3

Camouflage and Concealment Techniques.

Camouflage and concealment techniques are not decorative, they are essential tactical tools for stealth, survival, and the element of surprise.

Knowing how to camouflage properly allows a player to observe without being seen, to move undetected, and to position themselves in key locations without alerting the enemy.

Camouflage is not just about clothing, it's a strategy that involves how you move, how you position yourself on the terrain, and how you adapt your silhouette and visual presence to the environment.

Blending effectively into the field turns a player into a ghost, someone who is present but whom no one can locate until it's too late.

The first principle is understanding that camouflage must be adapted to the specific environment of the game.

There is no universal pattern that works in all terrains.

A multicam pattern may be very effective in a dry forest or mixed terrain, but it stands out in an urban concrete environment.

A traditional woodland camo works very well in dense vegetation, but it becomes conspicuous in open areas or fields with little shade.

That's why a player who takes concealment seriously doesn't choose their uniform based on aesthetics, but on functionality.

They study the playing field before the match, analyze the dominant colors, the density of vegetation, the textures of the ground, and choose their clothing accordingly.

Some even modify their uniforms by adding pieces of fabric, netting, or natural elements to break up the monotony of the pattern.

The use of a ghillie suit is an advanced example of concealment.

It's a garment specifically designed to completely break up the human silhouette, using strips of fabric, synthetic fibers, or even real vegetation tied to the uniform.

A sniper wearing a well-made ghillie suit can lie down five meters from an enemy patrol without being detected, as long as they don't move.

But it's not enough to just put it on—you have to know how to craft and adapt it.

The ghillie suit used in a green forest cannot be the same as one for arid terrain.

Many players collect leaves, dry branches, or grass from the field just before the game and integrate them into the suit to achieve perfect blending with the environment.

They also make sure the fibers aren't too reflective or uniform, as light can give them away.

Beyond clothing, real camouflage begins with the silhouette.

The human eye is trained to detect familiar shapes, and the human silhouette, whether standing or crouching, is one of the easiest to identify.

That's why effective camouflage involves changing the shape

of the body: breaking up straight lines, eliminating defined edges, and avoiding contrast.

A well-camouflaged player does not place themselves directly against a smooth background (like a white wall or a flat rock), because their shape stands out due to contrast.

Instead, they position themselves next to irregularly textured objects, such as bushes, mounds of earth, trees with exposed roots, or piles of debris.

If they also remain still and control their breathing, they can go completely unnoticed even in relatively open areas.

Stillness is a key aspect, because no matter how good a player's camouflage is, if they move at the wrong moment, their presence becomes obvious.

Movement is what gives away a player the most on the field.

That's why those who master concealment move slowly, with control, and only when the environment allows it: when there is ambient noise, when the enemy is distracted, or when there are intermediate cover points.

Some players advance literally centimeter by centimeter over several minutes, crawling on their stomachs and using the terrain as natural cover.

If they're in tall grass, they learn to push it gently so it doesn't draw attention; if they're among branches, they know how to move them without causing sudden vibrations.

Another important aspect of concealment is the management of shine and reflections.

Many players give themselves away by not properly covering their gear.

Scopes with lenses that reflect sunlight, shiny barrels,

protective goggles without anti-reflective treatment, or even very clean plastic patches can be visible from dozens of meters away if hit by direct sunlight.

Experienced players wrap their replicas with camouflage tape, paint metal parts with matte paint, and place small nets or covers over their optics.

Some even cover their goggles with fine mesh veils that don't interfere with vision but prevent the lenses from catching light.

Sound is also part of camouflage, as a silent player is much more likely to stay concealed than one who makes noise while moving.

Equipment must be tightly secured, with no loose parts clanking together, magazines, keys, carabiners, or metal items should be padded or stowed inside the vest.

Even breathing can be adjusted: heavy breathing reveals nervousness, and a sharp-eared enemy can hear it from just a few meters away in enclosed environments.

Well-trained players practice moving silently: they know that stepping on dry leaves, snapping twigs, or loose gravel can ruin all their camouflage.

A player who manages to move undetected for twenty or thirty minutes and reaches a key position where they can observe or eliminate an enemy leader without ever being seen has applied camouflage to its highest expression.

4.4

Reaction to Enemy Contact.

Reaction to enemy contact is one of the most critical moments a player or squad can face.

Everything that has been planned, trained, or anticipated can fall apart in seconds if the reaction is not quick, coordinated, and appropriate to the type of contact.

When an unexpected encounter with enemy forces occurs—whether visual, auditory, or direct fire—the way you respond will determine the difference between surviving and being eliminated, advancing or getting pinned down, regaining control or falling into panic.

There is no room for clumsy improvisation.

Reacting correctly requires reflexes, communication, environmental awareness, and most importantly, having internalized a tactical response structure that can be executed almost automatically.

The first thing that happens in a contact situation is detection.

You might see a shadow move between the trees, hear a distant shot, or feel a burst of fire whistling overhead.

The most common mistake at this moment is to freeze, peek without thinking, or shoot without a visual on the target.

A well-trained player doesn't panic: they crouch or drop to the ground, identify the direction of fire (by sound, impact, or their teammates' reactions), and immediately seek real cover.

Here, every second counts.

The player who stays out in the open trying to figure out "where it came from" will likely be the first to go down.

In contrast, the one who immediately pulls back, turns their body to cover the flanks, and relocates behind a log, a rock, or a corner already has a tactical advantage.

The next phase is communication.

If the contact was visual, the player must relay it clearly and concisely: "Two enemies, left flank, near the dead tree, 30 meters."

If it was due to incoming fire without visual confirmation, they should indicate the direction relative to the team: "We're taking fire from the front, 12 o'clock, take cover now."

The squad leader or radio operator can then respond accordingly, whether by ordering a retreat, initiating suppressive fire, or deploying a flanking pair.

This step is crucial: if each player acts independently without communicating, the team becomes disorganized, overlaps lines of fire, or exposes itself unnecessarily.

An immediate tactical response often includes suppressive fire.

Even without a visual on the enemy, sending a burst toward the area where the attack came from can force the enemy to stop, seek better cover, or lose the initiative.

This is known as "suppressive fire."

It's not about shooting randomly, it's about directing fire at a specific area to stop the enemy's advance.

For example, if a team is being attacked from a ruined house, the player with a direct line of sight lays down constant fire on the windows while their teammates reposition or flank.

In many cases, this simple act prevents the enemy from peeking out and allows your squad to regain control of the area.

If contact occurs at close range and the enemy already has the advantage, the only options are to maneuver aggressively or retreat in an orderly fashion.

The most effective maneuver in this context is "fire and movement": while one player fires, the other moves, then they switch roles.

This is done in pairs: one provides cover while the other moves to a better position or falls back.

This prevents everyone from being trapped behind the same cover or running at the same time and being easily hit.

This principle also applies during an advance: if the enemy is spotted but the squad decides to push forward, one group maintains suppressive fire while another flanks to attack from the blind side.

It's a game of quick decisions, moving without cover is suicidal; staying still for too long is just as dangerous.

In CQB situations, such as encounters inside buildings or hallways, the reaction must be even more immediate.

Here, contact can be sudden, at just a few meters, with no time to plan.

The player who reacts best is the one who already has their replica raised, aiming at expected areas and advancing with a "foot peek," exposing just enough to see without revealing their whole body.

If an enemy appears at a hallway intersection, the ideal response is to quickly fall back, throw a sound grenade or BB grenade (if allowed), or change angles to force an engagement under better conditions.

Shooting without thinking or yelling can alert nearby enemies.

Reaction also involves adaptability.

Sometimes, the best response to enemy contact is not immediate return fire, but stealth.

For example, if you're on an infiltration mission and detect an enemy patrol but haven't been seen yet, not opening fire might be the smartest choice.

You slowly withdraw, change your route, and maintain the element of surprise.

Many players ruin operations by firing at the first target they see, without considering the overall mission.

A well-trained sniper, for instance, might observe for several minutes before deciding whether to shoot or not, carefully weighing whether revealing their position is worth it.

It's also important to stay calm.

During contact, adrenaline spikes, vision narrows, movements become rushed, and aim can falter.

The best players are those who control that impulse, breathe, aim steadily, and act with intention.

A very clear example is when a squad is advancing along a path and a single enemy shot from the side takes out the lead player.

Beginners scatter, shoot wildly, or drop to the ground without coordination.

A trained team, on the other hand, splits into two—one lays down suppressive fire while the other executes a U-shaped maneuver to eliminate the threat.

All in under thirty seconds.

4.5

Active Surveillance and Use of the Senses.

This is an aspect many players underestimate, especially those more focused on shooting than observing.

But the player who masters their senses and maintains conscious awareness of their surroundings has a constant tactical advantage, even without firing a single BB.

Being alert is not just looking without seeing, or hearing without listening; it's about interpreting what's happening around you, anticipating movements, detecting patterns, and reading the field as if it were a living map.

It means having your eyes and ears more active than your trigger finger.

Active surveillance begins long before contact with the enemy.

As soon as the player enters the field, they should start registering details of the terrain: where the covers are, the high points, escape routes, natural choke points, obstacles, open areas, and blind spots.

This is done constantly and almost automatically.

With every step, the player analyzes: if I get shot at from that hill, where do I run? If I need to flank, how do I do it without being exposed?

That tactical awareness before action is what allows quick and effective decisions when the game intensifies.

The Sense of Sight Is the Most Obvious, but Also the Most

Overloaded.

It's not just about looking straight ahead, but about constantly scanning the surroundings.

The eyes should move from left to right, from near to far, detecting movement, contrasts, and out-of-place colors.

A lens reflection, a metallic glint, a slight shift in a shadow, or the movement of a branch in a windless environment can give away an enemy's position.

You're not looking for a full human figure, you're looking for clues, anomalies.

For example, if you're in a wooded area and see a shadow with a perfectly straight line in the middle of the foliage—a replica barrel sticking out—you know someone is there.

A good player doesn't stare at a single fixed point; they sweep their gaze like they're scanning a document.

They learn to look between objects, not just at them.

Hearing Is Just as Important, If Not More

Many contacts are detected by sound before they are seen.

An experienced player can distinguish a branch snapping under a boot, the click of a fire selector, the hum of an AEG motor starting up, the soft knock of a magazine against a vest, or the whisper of an unsecured radio transmission.

In intense matches, when everyone is shooting, these sounds get drowned out, but in moments of silence, a single misstep can give away an ambush.

That's why attentive players stop from time to time, not just to rest, but to listen.

Five seconds of total silence can tell you more than blindly advancing twenty meters.

Touch also plays a subtle but real role.

Feeling the vibration of the ground as a heavy enemy squad approaches, noticing tension in the trigger, or sensing the moisture of the terrain to choose a better place to support yourself and avoid slipping.

For example, if a player is crawling over dry ground and suddenly feels the surface change to wet soil, they'll know they're in an area where they might leave a trace.

That awareness prompts them to change their route or adjust the way they move.

Touch also applies to weapon handling: knowing if the fire selector is properly set, sensing a BB jam without having to look, or detecting through vibration that the magazine's hopper has emptied.

Even smell can play a role, albeit a minor one.

In prolonged matches, the scent of gas from a GBB can reveal that an enemy fired nearby, or the smell of a smoke grenade can give you a clue about where an assault is coming from.

Active surveillance also means observing your own team, knowing where your teammates are, what they're covering, and who's flanking.

If one of them raises a hand without speaking or makes a gesture, you must pick up on it and process it instantly.

If you see a teammate staring at a fixed point for more than three seconds, they may have spotted something.

A good player doesn't just watch the enemy, they monitor the entire situation, like an omnipresent observer.

A clear example: a squad is advancing along a wooded path.

The rear player hears a branch snap to their left.

They see nothing, but they communicate: "Light movement, sector 9." Everyone stops.

The leader scans the area and notices a faint reflection.

They send the DMR to cover the flank, and in under a minute, they've contained an ambush before it happens.

That wasn't luck, it was the result of constant attention and active surveillance.

The key to active surveillance is to never "disconnect."

Many players relax after ten minutes without contact, they let their guard down, start chatting, look at the ground, or simply lose focus.

That's exactly when it's easiest to fall into a trap.

A good player keeps their mind sharp like a radar, always sensing, interpreting, and anticipating.

They're not paranoid, they're in control.

Chapter 5: Squad and Unit Strategies

5.1

Patrol and Column Formations.

Patrol and column formations are a fundamental technique for moving as a unit across the field, especially in scenarios that require travel through open terrain, wooded areas, narrow routes, or under limited visibility conditions.

These formations are not just military formalities adapted to gameplay, they are functional structures that help maintain cohesion, cover sectors, prevent ambushes, and respond effectively to enemy contact.

A poorly formed, scattered, or disorganized patrol is easy to ambush and difficult to coordinate; a well-formed patrol is a mobile tactical body that adapts to the terrain and protects its members at all times.

The most common and versatile formation in airsoft is the column, also called "single file."

It is mainly used in tight areas such as forest paths, narrow corridors, routes between walls, or poorly defined trails.

In this formation, players walk one behind the other, with a safe distance of one to two meters between them, depending on the environment and the risk of contact.

The lead player, known as the "point man," is responsible for guiding the patrol, scanning the front, and making initial decisions in case of detection or contact.

Right behind them is usually the squad leader or navigator, who directs the general orientation.

In the middle of the formation is where the main firepower is placed: assaulters, support, and the medic if there is one.

At the rear, the formation is closed by the "rear guard" or "tail," who is responsible for covering the six (the group's back) and detecting any possible pursuit or threats from behind.

This player must be extremely alert, as they are the first to detect a rear ambush.

The advantage of the column is that it offers a very low profile to the enemy when moving stealthily.

However, its main weakness is that in the event of frontal contact, the group is lined up with limited immediate response capability.

That's why this formation is often quickly transformed into another more suitable one if there's suspicion of nearby enemies.

A common transition is from column to "line formation" (all players side by side) to maximize the firing front, or into a "V formation" to advance while covering more angles.

Another useful tactical setup is the "wedge formation" or "inverted V," in which the leader or point man is at the front and the rest fan out diagonally to the flanks.

This is ideal for advancing through open or wooded terrain with moderate visibility, as it allows for flank coverage and gives each player a clear firing angle to the front and sides.

It's slower and requires greater control, but it is effective for detecting threats before being detected.

Additionally, in the event of an ambush, this formation allows for immediate dispersion toward lateral cover.

The wedge is typical in reconnaissance patrols or in the

phases leading up to an assault.

For example, if a squad is patrolling a wooded area with the possibility of mid-range contact, an open wedge allows two or three players to simultaneously detect enemy movement and open fire in a fan pattern.

The "line formation" (everyone advancing side by side) is useful for clearing an area, such as dense forest or open field, where a frontal offensive is required.

In this formation, each player has a clear field of fire to the front and toward the opposite flank of their teammate, allowing the entire visual field to be constantly covered.

However, its weakness is the rear, if the group is ambushed from behind or from a flank, reorganization is slow.

For that reason, the players on the far right and far left must constantly turn their heads and monitor the full 180° field of view.

The "diamond formation" is more commonly used during protection movements, such as escorts or extraction missions.

Four players form a closed shape around an element in the center (such as a hostage, VIP, or wounded player) and move while covering all angles: front, rear, and both flanks.

It's slow but extremely secure when executed with proper synchronization.

In milsim scenarios, where players must rescue objects, people, or escort symbolic elements, this formation is essential to prevent the enemy from exploiting gaps in the group's coverage.

During patrols, managing pace and silence is also vital,

as the team must advance with measured steps, avoiding unnecessary noise and using prearranged signals.

Communication is done through gestures: a raised hand to stop, a closed fist to hold position, two fingers pointing to the eyes to indicate visual contact, a downward-facing palm to advance silently, or a punch in the air to initiate a deployment.

Voices are only used when contact is unavoidable or when immediate orders must be given.

Another key rule in patrol formations is the use of "sectors of responsibility."

Each player is assigned an angle they must constantly monitor.

The point man looks forward, the second slightly to the right, the third to the left, and so on.

This prevents the entire team from looking in the same direction and allows for full 360° coverage.

While moving, each player watches their sector as if their life depends on it.

If a player fails to monitor their sector, that gap can be exploited by a flanking enemy, a hidden sniper, or a rival patrol passing undetected.

Lastly, an effective patrol doesn't just walk, it stops, listens, observes, and moves again.

"Tactical halts" allow the group to rest, regain visibility, and avoid falling into predictable movement patterns.

For example, every 50 meters or at each change in terrain, the leader can give the signal to stop.

Everyone crouches or remains still for 15 seconds.

In that silence, they can detect movement, adjust positions, or reassess direction.

An alert enemy might detect a group by the rhythm of their footsteps, but if that rhythm is broken with unexpected pauses, the group gains an advantage.

5.2

Offensive Maneuvers:
Fire and Advance, Flanking, Pincer.

Offensive maneuvers are fundamental techniques that allow a team to break through a defense, regain the initiative, and gain ground without resorting to unnecessary frontal combat.

The three most effective and commonly used maneuvers in this context are fire and advance, flanking, and the pincer maneuver.

Each one requires a high level of coordination, communication, and tactical discipline, and when executed correctly, even a small team can disorganize and defeat a larger or better-positioned opponent.

The fire and advance maneuver, also known as fire and movement, is the foundation of any tactical offensive.

It involves advancing toward an enemy position by alternating between covering fire and movement.

While one or more players fire to keep the enemy's head down, their teammates advance toward the objective.

Once those advancing players reach new cover, they take over the suppressive fire so the others can move up.

This sequence is repeated in a synchronized manner, allowing the entire group to advance under constant protection.

The success of this technique lies in discipline: the player who is firing must not move until the other is covering, and vice versa.

A common mistake is having everyone move at the same time, exposing themselves unnecessarily.

For example, if a squad spots an enemy holed up in a house, two players can maintain constant fire on the windows while the other two move between cover, closing the distance.

Then, roles are switched, and the group manages to reach a position from which they can enter the building or flank it.

Flanking is one of the most effective maneuvers to destabilize the enemy without engaging them head-on.

It consists of attacking from a lateral or rear angle, taking advantage of the enemy's blind spot.

For a flank to be successful, it's crucial to identify the direction of enemy fire, locate weak points in the perimeter, and move stealthily to a favorable position.

While part of the team pins the enemy from the front, one or two players move off to the side of the field—ideally using vegetation, structures, or terrain features for cover—until they reach a spot where the enemy isn't expecting them.

From there, they open fire or directly infiltrate the enemy's rear.

For example, in a wooded terrain match, a squad is taking fire from a hill.

Instead of pushing from the front, two players move to the left, using a line of trees, and appear at the enemy's flank, who was focused on firing forward.

Within seconds, they manage to eliminate them or force them to retreat.

The pincer maneuver, also known as "double flanking" or

"clamp attack," is a more complex and powerful version of the flank.

It consists of attacking the enemy simultaneously from both flanks while another part of the team keeps them occupied from the front.

The goal is to encircle them, force them to split their attention, and cut off their escape routes, ultimately leading to their collapse.

This tactic requires more players and greater coordination, but it is extremely effective in open or semi-urban environments.

A clear example would be an enemy squad entrenched in an L-shaped structure.

The attacking team splits its forces: one group advances from the front, delivering intermittent fire to hold the enemy's attention, while two other groups move around the position, one from each side.

Once the flanks are in position, a signal is given, and all groups attack simultaneously.

The enemy finds themselves surrounded, lacking sufficient cover, and with little time to reorganize.

The pincer maneuver doesn't just aim to eliminate, it aims to collapse the opponent's tactical morale, forcing them to retreat or surrender.

All of these offensive maneuvers require three key elements: timing, communication, and knowledge of the terrain.

Timing refers to choosing the right moment to execute them, too early, and the enemy may detect you; too late, and they might have reinforced their position.

Communication is essential to know when to initiate the maneuver, how to synchronize fire, and who is covering whom.

It's not enough to just shoot, you need to coordinate who is laying down fire, who is moving, and when to change tactics if the maneuver fails.

Finally, knowledge of the terrain allows you to identify approach routes, cover, obstacles, and potential detection points.

You can't flank if you don't know what's on the other side of the wall or what kind of terrain lies beyond the forest.

Additionally, maneuvers must be adapted to the number of players, the type of replica, and the environment.

A small group of three players can execute a basic fire and advance if they take proper turns.

A six-player team can perform an effective pincer if organized into trios.

The player carrying a heavy support weapon might be the key to pinning the enemy from the front, while assaulters with lighter replicas move along the flanks.

Even weather or time of day can have an impact: in night games, a flank can be more aggressive; in open terrain under full sunlight, a pincer must be executed with greater caution.

5.3

**Position Defense:Trenches,
Buildings, and Choke Points.**

Defending positions is a tactical discipline in itself.

It's not just about "waiting for the enemy," but about knowing
how to turn the terrain to your advantage, anticipating enemy
attack routes, managing fields of fire, and holding effectively
under pressure.

Whether defending trenches, buildings, or choke points,
the success of a defense lies in preparation, team distribution,
fire discipline, and the ability to withstand and counterattack at
the right moment.

A good defense is not static, it is flexible, layered, and active.

Defending trenches involves maximizing their linear cover and
low profile.

Well-constructed trenches allow players to fire from low
positions, keep their silhouette hidden, and move from
one point to another without exposing themselves.

The key is not to overcrowd them.

Many make the mistake of lining up five or six players in the
same firing lane, which makes them vulnerable to grenades,
flanking, or concentrated fire.

The best practice is to place spaced-out shooters with
overlapping fields of support, and position a player with
a light machine gun at the center or in the best angle of fire.

For example, in an L-shaped trench, you can assign one

player to each arm and one at the intersection with an LMG to cover frontal movement.

Another player should stay in the rear as a backup or to maintain contact with the rest of the team.

In trenches, fire should also be measured: prolonged bursts reveal your position and deplete ammunition.

The most effective method is to fire in short bursts, cover your assigned sectors, and reposition between trench segments to avoid being spotted from a single angle.

Defending buildings requires discipline and control over entry points. It's not about filling every window with a player, but about prioritizing entrances, staircases, and possible breach points.

The biggest mistake when defending a house is having everyone focus on the windows while leaving doors unguarded.

The most effective setup is to place just one or two observers on the upper floors, while the rest defend from within, hidden in the shadows, ready to block hallways or repel intrusions.

A door can be covered from a lateral angle, outside the attacker's line of sight, allowing the defender to eliminate them before being seen.

If there are stairs, defenders should be positioned at the top, not directly at the landing, but halfway up, behind a railing or low wall for cover.

In a typical urban assault, when the enemy tries to enter the first floor, a defender hidden in an adjacent room can throw a flashbang or open concentrated fire that completely disrupts the advance.

Additionally, windows should be used intermittently: shoot, move away, switch to another window.

An alert enemy will know that if you always shoot from the same frame, they can aim at it the moment you appear.

Choke points—hallways, narrow doorways, alleys, corridors between walls—are areas of absolute control when used correctly.

Their main strength is that they limit the number of attackers who can advance at once, forcing them to move one by one or peek gradually.

But they also have a weakness: if the defender is spotted and can't move, they become a static target.

That's why defending a choke point must allow for alternation and mobility.

If a player is covering a hallway from a corner, they should have a second nearby piece of cover to fall back to under pressure.

A staggered defense can also be used: one player in front and another behind, ready to take over if the first is taken out or needs to reload.

In long hallways, an effective tactic is to place obstacles (barricades, chairs, barrels) to slow the enemy's advance, force them to expose themselves longer, and gain valuable seconds to shoot or call for support.

For example, in a CQB tournament, a player was defending a door leading to a 15-meter corridor.

He placed a table 7 meters in as a distraction and a trap grenade just behind it.

When the first attacker crouched to use the table as cover, he triggered the grenade and was eliminated before he could fire.

Defense also includes knowing when not to shoot.

If an enemy hasn't detected you yet, but you're in a key position, opening fire too early can compromise the entire setup.

Sometimes, it's better to let them pass, wait for them to move deeper into the area, and eliminate them from a position of advantage.

This is known as active passive defense, letting the enemy overextend so they walk into a crossfire zone.

A solid defense also means always having an escape or repositioning route.

No position is impenetrable, and if the enemy advances with grenades, coordinated fire, or superior numbers, the best option may be to fall back to a second defensive point.

This requires prior planning, a retreat can't be improvised once you're already surrounded.

That's why, in well-organized matches, leaders designate two or three fallback defensive positions, allowing the squad to retreat in an orderly manner.

A classic example: defend a building, then fall back to defend the backyard, and finally retreat to an extraction point or elevated zone.

It's also essential to rotate defenders, because if a player has been covering the same corner or window for 15 minutes, their focus drops, their vision adjusts to the pattern, and they become vulnerable.

Switching positions, even with another teammate, refreshes vigilance and prevents the enemy from identifying a presence pattern.

5.4

Ambushes and Counterattacks.

Ambushes and counterattacks are advanced offensive and defensive tactics that, when executed precisely, can radically alter the course of a match.

A well-planned ambush doesn't just eliminate the enemy: it causes disarray, sows fear, breaks cohesion, and forces retreat or critical mistakes.

An effective counterattack, on the other hand, is a tactical response to enemy pressure or assault that turns a defensive situation into an unexpected offensive.

Both require planning, synchronization, terrain awareness, and emotional control.

An ambush is a planned offensive action launched from a concealed position, aimed at surprising and neutralizing the enemy at their most vulnerable moment and location.

For it to work, favorable terrain must be chosen: a narrow pass, a path with high edges, a dense vegetation zone, a blind curve, or a natural bottleneck.

The key is that the enemy has no way of anticipating the presence of the ambushing group until it's too late.

Success relies on the element of surprise, concentrated fire, and the enemy's inability to respond or maneuver in the first seconds.

A classic example is an ambush set along a forest trail.

Players are positioned on both sides, parallel to the path,

about 5 to 10 meters away.

When the enemy patrol enters the kill zone—ideally when its midpoint is centered—a signal is given (it can be a single shot, a radio command, or a hand gesture), and fire is opened simultaneously from both sides.

In less than five seconds, most of the patrol is neutralized or completely thrown into disarray.

If the last player is intentionally allowed to escape, it can serve as a channel to spread a sense of insecurity and weaken the enemy team's morale.

The key to an effective ambush is not just accurate shooting but proper placement of each operator.

The flanks must close the trap, the center must control the flow, and there should always be a second group positioned further back, ready to intercept anyone trying to escape or counterattack.

Maintaining absolute silence before contact is also critical.

Positions should not be given away through unnecessary movement, talking, or premature shots.

In milsim or night games, sights are even covered with tape to avoid reflections, and communication is done through prearranged hand signals.

Discipline is everything: firing too early ruins the ambush.

An ambush can also be defensive.

For example, faking a retreat or exposing a weak position to lure the enemy into a prepared area, where another group lies in wait in silence.

This is known as "bait."

Let's say an enemy squad is advancing aggressively toward a position.

Two players pretend to retreat, showing signs of panic or disorder, guiding the enemy into a narrow corridor where a duo equipped with heavy support and grenades is waiting to eliminate them with crossfire.

This "lure" ambush is highly effective, especially against inexperienced players who get caught up in the thrill of the chase.

A counterattack, on the other hand, is an offensive maneuver launched from a defensive position immediately after halting or resisting an enemy assault.

Its purpose is not just to respond, but to seize the initiative at the exact moment when the enemy is weakened, falling back, reorganizing, or reloading.

It requires cold blood, tactical awareness, and a perfect sense of the battle's tempo.

The right moment to counterattack is not at the first shot, but when it becomes clear that the enemy has lost momentum or made a mistake.

A clear example of a counterattack would be in an urban environment: the enemy has launched a frontal assault on a defended building.

After several minutes of intense fire, a pause is detected.

The defenders, instead of waiting for another attack, execute a quick breakout through the side door, take the street, and strike the attacking group from the rear while they're still recovering, reloading, or seeking cover.

This action completely reverses the dynamic and forces the enemy to defend themselves at a moment when they're not prepared to do so.

The counterattack can also take the form of a flank maneuver.

If the enemy has focused too heavily in one direction and leaves a side exposed, a quick-response team can silently move along that flank and attack from an unexpected position.

This requires always keeping a small reserve team in the rear, without overcommitting all forces to the initial defense.

Ambushes and counterattacks can also be combined, for example, a team can simulate a failed ambush, retreat, and once the enemy grows overconfident and advances in disarray, launch a counterattack from a secondary position.

Alternatively, an ambush can be executed and, if it partially fails, the team can split and launch a counterattack from a second angle to close the trap.

A common element in both tactics is mastery of timing and terrain.

Without a good reading of the environment, it's impossible to know where to set an ambush or where to counterattack.

Without control of timing, the action is either too late or too early, before the enemy is truly committed.

Patience is vital: in an ambush, you may have to remain motionless in position for 20 minutes.

In a counterattack, you might need to hold out for several minutes before the exact moment arrives to strike back with full force.

5.5

Rescue, Hostage, and Extraction Simulations.

These scenarios aren't just about eliminating the enemy, they revolve around achieving objectives under pressure, coordinating teams, managing time, protecting a key element (a hostage or VIP), and ensuring their safe extraction from a hostile area.

These matches are often inspired by real-life special forces operations and require defined roles, clear command structures, and a strong dose of realism, where even communication errors can ruin the entire mission.

The most classic scenario is the rescue of a hostage held by enemy forces.

The "hostage" may be a neutral player or a symbolic object (a dummy, a briefcase, a canister with codes).

The attacking team must infiltrate the enemy's position, locate the target, verify its condition (sometimes, it can only be moved if "stabilized" by a tactical medic), and extract it to a pre-established safe zone.

Meanwhile, the defending team may have fortified the position, set traps, posted guards, or deployed quick reaction forces.

This type of mission isn't won by killing the enemy, it's won by extracting the target alive and within the time limit.

Pre-mission planning in this kind of match is essential.

The rescue team must be divided into sub-units:

An assault group to breach and secure the building, an external cover team to block reinforcements or intercept counterattacks, a tactical medic if the rules allow healing the hostage, and an extraction duo responsible for escorting the hostage once freed.

Pre-mission intelligence, such as terrain sketches, possible access routes, and extraction points, becomes a key part of success.

A squad leader with strategic vision might decide to launch a direct assault through a side window while another unit distracts the defenders at the main entrance.

The assault moment is one of maximum tension.

Defenders usually place the hostage in a central or hard-to-reach area and protect it from overlapping positions.

This forces the attacking team to clear the building room by room, use smoke or flash grenades, and coordinate double or multiple entries from different angles.

Often, special rules prohibit shooting the hostage: if they are accidentally hit, the mission fails.

This means attackers must be extremely precise, control their aggression, and prioritize identification before firing.

Once the target has been located, the most dangerous phase begins: the extraction.

This is where the most common mistakes occur, as some teams manage to free the hostage but fail to secure the escape route.

When the enemy realizes this, they counterattack and ambush during the transfer.

That's why a good team doesn't just assault, it maintains a mobile reserve, covers all sectors, and keeps watch on the flanks during the evacuation.

If the extraction zone is far away or in open ground, it may be necessary to create a "security corridor," in which two lines of fire are opened to allow safe passage for the duo escorting the hostage.

If the enemy has had time to regroup, the extraction team may have to improvise a new route, which requires terrain knowledge and immediate adaptability.

A variation of this mission is the timed rescue or detonator scenario.

For example, the hostage wears a vest with a timer or a fake bomb attached.

The medic must reach them and deactivate or remove it within a certain timeframe.

In other versions, extraction can only take place if certain codes, keys, or devices scattered across the field have been recovered beforehand.

This turns the match into a simultaneous tactical and intelligence operation, where every minute counts, and information can be more valuable than gunfire.

There are also missions where the "hostage" is an armed and cooperative VIP, who can walk but not shoot, or who can only use a pistol.

In this case, the team must protect them constantly, covering their movements, rotating their position, and ensuring they don't get exposed.

A frontal attack that kills the VIP results in immediate defeat.

This requires the team to move like a protective bubble, anticipate threats, and adjust their pace to match the movement of the objective.

Formations like the "diamond" or "tight column" are often used, where the VIP is positioned in the center and the escorts cover 360° with assigned sectors.

In urban environments, this becomes extremely intense, every corner can hide an attacker, every window could be a trap.

The defending team also has its own tactics.

They don't always bunker down.

Some defend actively: placing external patrols, lookouts at elevated points, and quick reaction squads.

A common method is to fake weakness in one area to lure the rescuers in, then spring a trap from the flanks.

If the hostage is mobile, some defenders will even move them constantly from room to room to disorient the enemy.

In longer matches, the defenders may use decoys, objects that resemble the hostage, to confuse or waste the attackers' time.

The level of realism in these simulations can go very far.

In milsim, the "hostage" may have an active role: shouting, resisting, or holding information that is only revealed if questioned properly.

They might even fake an injury and require a simulated bandage.

In these matches, combat is only one part of the whole.

Strategy, negotiation, resource management, and decision-making become just as important.

In one match, for example, the rescue team managed to get in without firing a single shot, using disguises and distractions to pose as allies.

They successfully retrieved the hostage and extracted them before anyone opened fire.

It was a total victory without a single casualty.

5.6

Terrain Study: Map Analysis, Key Points, Access Routes, and Visibility.

Terrain study is one of the most strategic and least flashy skills, yet also one of the most decisive for the success of an operation.

Knowing the field before the game begins is like entering a chess match already knowing how your opponents will move.

It's not just about "having played there before," but about analyzing maps, identifying key points, anticipating access routes, studying visibility zones, and designing movement and cover paths.

The player or squad that masters the terrain holds a constant tactical advantage, even before the first shot is fired.

The first step is map analysis.

If a layout of the field is available (which is often provided in milsim games or large events), the team should study it as a real commander would: examining the terrain features, lines of sight, elevated positions, wooded areas, structures, walkable paths, and the field boundaries.

A well-read map allows for the detection of natural chokepoints—places the enemy will be forced to pass through—as well as less obvious alternative routes.

For example, a team that notices a river with a single bridge between the enemy spawn and an objective will know that this point will be critical both for blocking and for ambushing.

On the other hand, another group may spot a ditch along the

side of the map, less guarded and ideal for a silent flank.

The next step is identifying the key points of the terrain.

These are locations that, if controlled, provide visual, strategic, or movement advantages.

For example, a central hill from which almost the entire field can be observed, a tall building that overlooks an urban zone, or a road intersection that leads to three or more critical areas.

These points are natural objectives for control or defense, but they are also highly contested zones.

Controlling them not only provides a better position but often allows for launching offensives or cutting off supply or reinforcement lines.

A team that places a DMR in a tower with a 180° view doesn't just shoot, they deny the enemy access to an entire sector.

Next come the access routes, so each team must map out not only the most direct path, but also the safest and quietest one, since often the shortest route is the most exposed, and the longer route the most effective.

For example, a group might choose to avoid the gravel path running through the center of the field and instead use an old, dry canal covered in vegetation that runs parallel to the forest.

They'll take five minutes longer, but they'll reach the enemy's flank undetected.

These types of secondary routes, also known as "infiltration lines," are incredibly valuable in reconnaissance, rescue, or flanking missions.

A team with strong terrain awareness doesn't move in straight lines, it moves in layers, combining speed, cover, and stealth.

One of the most underestimated factors in terrain study
is visibility, because it's not enough to know where you are,
you have to know who can see you, from where, and when.

Sunlight, terrain angle, vegetation height, and the density of
structures all directly affect the ability to detect or be detected.

A player may think they're well concealed in the bushes, but if
the sun is behind them and casts their shadow into a clearing,
they're giving away their position.

Or if they move along a ridge at dawn, their silhouette stands
out against the sky, making them an obvious target.

Visibility changes with weather, time of day, and orientation.

That's why experienced players analyze terrain in terms of
blind spots and lines of fire, they know from which points they
can observe without being seen, and from where their replica
can cover wide areas without exposure.

Terrain study also includes identifying risk zones, such as
open spaces with no cover, areas with multiple undefendable
access points, or positions that can be easily surrounded.

A clearing between two wooded zones might seem like the
fastest way to reach an objective, but if enemy spotters are
positioned along the edges, it becomes a "killbox", a deadly
trap.

A building with an unsecured rear can be taken by surprise
from the back if the full map wasn't properly studied.

Players who advance without this prior analysis fall into
ambushes repeatedly.

In contrast, a team that anticipates knows when to flank,

when to stop, when to advance at night, or when to wait for smoke cover.

In long-range matches, physically scouting the terrain before the game (if allowed) is also vital: walking it, testing cover, identifying areas where sound echoes more, or where the ground, like mud or gravel, can betray movement.

In milsim or multi-hour events, some teams mark reference points on the map with code names: "Alpha point," "tractor hill," "church corridor," so they can communicate quickly without needing to explain: "we're going to the second house at the end, the one with a tree."

That way, during gameplay, quick orders can be given: "support to Alpha 2, sniper takes the church, extraction at Wolf 3."

Finally, terrain study also applies to the defensive phase, knowing which sectors are likely to be attacked first, from which direction the enemy is most likely to approach, and what lines of cover exist between your position and theirs.

This allows you to place traps, establish crossfire zones, or set up early surveillance.

A team that defends without studying the terrain only reacts; but a team that studies the terrain anticipates.

5.7

**How to Adapt Strategy According to the Environment:
Forest, Urban, Desert, Industrial.**

Each type of environment—forest, urban, desert,
or industrial—imposes unique conditions that affect
visibility, movement, communication, cover, game tempo,
and even the effectiveness of certain roles or equipment.

A player or team that enters an environment applying generic
tactics, without adjusting their playstyle to the specific features
of the terrain, is clearly at a disadvantage compared to those
who have trained, observed, and designed their approach
specifically for that type of combat.

In forested terrain, the key lies in stealth, observation, and the
smart use of vegetation.

Camouflage becomes critically important, as a motionless
player in a good ghillie suit can remain unnoticed even at
close range.

Visibility is limited, so engagements tend to happen at
medium range, often with visual interruptions.

Movement must be silent, stepping on dry leaves, branches,
or stones can give away your position.

Movement is done slowly, in pairs, with frequent tactical
pauses to listen and observe.

The sniper and designated marksman are highly effective,
as long as they position themselves on natural elevations,
clearings with cover, or near mandatory transit zones.

Ambushes are highly effective when set along paths or

narrow passageways.

A squad defending in a forest must be staggered in formation, never in a straight line, and must cover all 360 degrees: the enemy can appear from any direction.

Conversely, when attacking, natural routes, ditches, and the topography should be used to approach without being seen.

In an urban environment (CQB or semi-urban), priorities shift drastically: here, speed, constant communication, and control of tight angles dominate.

Combat is close-quarters, sudden, and every corner can be a trap.

The use of compact replicas (submachine guns, short carbines), pistols, and grenades becomes essential.

Players must learn to clear rooms, cover staircases, and move along walls while always keeping their replica raised.

Formations in pairs or trios are essential, and roles become more fluid.

There's no time to move alone or spend minutes observing, action must be fast, but smart.

Crossfire is highly effective: placing one player on an upper floor and another on the ground level can turn a house into a fortress.

Squad work should focus on controlling access points, doors, windows, and stairways.

For example, if a squad wants to take a defended house, a good strategy is to throw a flashbang on the ground floor while executing a simultaneous entry through the rear and the staircase.

The use of decoys, smoke, or sound distractions is also common to force the enemy to reveal their positions.

In desert or open-field environments, visibility is nearly total, but cover is scarce.

This forces players to use the terrain intelligently: any dip, low wall, or abandoned structure becomes valuable.

Camouflage here isn't vegetative but based on color and silhouette, clothing must break up the human shape against arid backgrounds.

Movement must be done with extreme caution and always under fire support.

Fire and movement tactics are essential, with groups alternating between shooting and advancing roles.

Long-range replicas dominate, so DMRs and heavy support gain prominence.

If the terrain is flat, advancing in broad daylight is risky, night routes or smoke cover must be planned.

A common example is seeing a team split into two, with one laying down suppressive fire from a hill while the other flanks through a side ditch for a surprise attack.

Defense in this environment relies on detecting the enemy before they get close and eliminating them at a distance.

That's why elevated positions and spotters with optics are critical.

The industrial environment, such as abandoned factories, container yards, or machinery zones, blends urban elements with complex structures.

Here, every room, hallway, or machinery area becomes a tactical point.

Combat can change in seconds: from a narrow corridor to an open space, from an iron staircase to a room with multiple entrances.

Communication must be fast and visual, radios are useful, but sometimes it's better to use hand signals due to sound reverberation.

The noise of metal structures can give away positions, so movements must be carefully planned.

Elevated positions (cranes, catwalks) are key for controlling wide areas, but they're also vulnerable if the player reveals their location.

Ambushes around corners, shots through narrow openings, or simultaneous entries from multiple doors are common.

The team must be divided with clear roles: one group advances, another secures the upper floor, and a third is responsible for sealing the perimeter.

For example, to take a hangar, a squad may deploy a smoke screen from the front entrance and then breach through a side gate while another player provides cover from a metal walkway.

Each environment forces you to rethink everything: what gear to bring, how to move, which roles to prioritize, how to communicate, and even what pace of play to adopt.

In the forest, the key is to stay hidden.

In urban settings, to clear quickly.

In the desert, to avoid exposure.

In industrial zones, to control heights and angles.

The team that understands this and adapts on the fly can dominate any terrain.

Because in airsoft, the environment is as much an enemy or ally as the opposing team, and only those who make it part of their strategy survive and win.

Chapter 6: Close Quarters Battle (CQB)

6.1

Room Entry and Clearing Techniques.

Close Quarters Battle (CQB) is one of the most intense, demanding, and technical disciplines in the game.

Here, everything happens in fractions of a second.

There is no room for clumsy improvisation or panic, decisions must be made automatically, based on training, coordination, and absolute trust in your teammate.

What is resolved with patience and distance in open-field combat is resolved in CQB with speed, surgical precision, and total mastery of short movements, indoor orientation, and room entry and clearing techniques.

Entry techniques are the core of any CQB operation.

A poor entry can mean the instant elimination of a player, or an entire squad.

The first fundamental principle is never to enter without a plan and support.

Before breaching a room, there must be a quick assessment: how many entrances there are, whether there are windows, what the approach angle is, whether enemies are suspected inside, and what kind of weapons are being carried.

The second principle is controlled speed: it's not about rushing in, but entering with determination, mutual cover, and without stopping until the position is secured.

There are several entry techniques depending on the situation.

The most basic is the (cross entry).

It's performed by two players: one enters and turns to the right, the other turns to the left, each covering their sector without interfering with each other or crossing lines of fire.

This allows both sides of the room to be cleared in under two seconds.

Each player must move without staying stationary, ideally following along the wall, and then occupy a secure point to cover from within.

If there are more than two players, the next ones enter and cover the center or elevated areas (windows, staircases, tall furniture).

This technique is ideal for square or medium-sized rooms with a single entry point.

Another common method is the (buttonhook entry), where both players enter and turn to the same side, forming an arc that clears a specific zone of the room.

It's useful when the enemy is suspected to be entrenched in a particular sector, or if the door opens in a direction that favors that angle.

However, it must be used with caution, as it leaves the opposite side momentarily uncovered.

In high-risk situations, a delayed entry can be used.

This involves opening the door, throwing in a flashbang, smoke, or BB grenade, and waiting a few seconds before entering.

This disorients the enemy and allows players to enter more safely.

The door can be opened silently (if possible) or pushed forcefully after a signal.

In intense CQB matches, it's common to train the first player to enter crouched, the second at a higher level, and the third to move directly toward the center if a hostage needs to be secured or the room cleared quickly.

A more advanced technique is entry from multiple points simultaneously.

If the room has two doors, two groups coordinate to breach at the same time from opposite sides, trapping the enemies in a crossfire.

This requires precise communication and a synchronized countdown, "Breaching in 3, 2, 1, now", followed by a simultaneous assault.

If radio communication isn't available, players use hand signals or knocks on the wall.

Upon entry, sectors of responsibility must be clearly defined.

Each player covers a specific angle: right, left, center, and any high or low zones if applicable.

No one crosses paths, no one hesitates, no one stays in the middle.

After entering, players must avoid standing in the line of fire from the doorway.

Many players make the mistake of shooting from the doorway frame or staying too close to the entrance, making them easy targets.

The proper method is to move in two or three steps, clear the area, and take up a lateral position from which they can provide cover without being exposed.

Room clearing doesn't end with eliminating visible enemies.

Blind spots must be checked: behind furniture, under beds, inside showers if it's a detailed urban scenario.

If the mission involves hostages or object retrieval, closets, hidden corners, or spaces under stairs must also be searched.

Extreme caution is needed when approaching new doors, never enter without checking first.

The "foot peek" or mirror technique is used (with a small angled mirror or a camera), or the replica is extended around the corner first with controlled aim.

The use of sound and body language is also essential.

Steps should be quiet, weapons held firmly without hitting walls or doors, and gestures should be clear and agreed upon: a closed fist for stop, open palm to advance, and fingers indicating number of enemies if something is spotted inside.

In matches where flashlights are allowed, they should be used with control: turned on briefly to "blind" and scan quickly, then turned off before becoming an easy target.

Players who master CQB train these techniques over and over.

They practice entries with mock doors, hallway clearing, L-shaped corner coverage, and coordination in tight spaces.

They know that in CQB, mistakes are costly, everything happens at 3 or 4 meters, and a poor entry can wipe out the entire team.

That's why discipline, mutual cover, and role clarity are prioritized: who enters first, who provides cover, who clears, and who gives the "clear" signal.

6.2

Shooting Priorities in Hallways and Corners.

Understanding and correctly applying shooting priorities in hallways and corners is essential for surviving in close quarters environments, especially in CQB combat, where most engagements happen at very short distances with very little reaction time.

Shooting priorities are not simply instinctive decisions; they are tactical protocols that determine which threats must be neutralized first based on their danger level, proximity, position, and visibility.

These decisions are made in seconds, and getting them right can save the player and the team.

Getting them wrong can mean being eliminated or allowing the enemy to take control of the space.

When clearing a hallway, the absolute priority is to control the deepest line of sight and cover any sector intersections.

A long hallway with multiple doors, alcoves, or side entries is a highly dangerous space, because any enemy hiding along its edges can fire from hard-to-cover angles.

Upon entering a hallway, the first player must always aim toward the far end, as that is the most distant and potentially dangerous zone.

The following players cover the sides and any doors along the way.

If everyone aims forward, they're left vulnerable to attacks from the sides.

If everyone focuses on the doors, any enemy at the far end has a clear line to eliminate them all in a row.

That's why the most common technique in hallways is sector distribution.

The first player covers the front, the second the right flank, the third the left, and the last watches the rear.

This formation allows for steady advancement while securing every angle, with slow movements and constant cover.

If movement is detected at the far end, the first player can open fire while the second and third move into side doorways to flank the enemy.

If contact is made from the side, the player closest to the threat responds while the others take supporting positions.

Corners are even more delicate, as peeking around one gradually exposes the player to a space that can't be fully seen in advance.

Here, the priority is to identify whether there are enemies visible and with a direct line of fire, even if they are farther away.

The most common mistake is to shoot at the nearest enemy simply because they're close, even if they don't have an angle, while ignoring a more distant one who does have a clear line of sight and is already aiming.

For example, if a player peeks around a corner and sees two enemies: one three meters away but facing the other direction, and another eight meters away aiming directly at them, the priority is to shoot the one farther away first.

The closer enemy can be taken out afterward with ease, but the one aiming down the hallway is an immediate threat.

Another fundamental technique is the "foot peek" or controlled peek.

Before revealing the head or body, many players expose a minimal part (like a foot or the barrel) to provoke enemy fire and thus pinpoint their exact location.

You can also slightly expose the shoulder or the replica's sight without compromising your head.

Once the enemy is detected, the next step is to peek out, fire, and retreat.

The key is not to stay at the corner for more than a second, any player who remains statically exposed becomes an immediate target.

The rhythm should be: peek – quick shot – cover – change angle – peek again.

This alternation keeps the enemy disoriented and prevents them from adapting to a movement pattern.

In "L-shaped corners" (where a hallway turns left or right), the shooting priority always belongs to the player on the inner side.

That means the player turning the corner is at a disadvantage, as they enter the field of view of an enemy who is already aiming.

That's why when turning a corner, it should be done with prior support, smoke grenade, a teammate aiming from another angle, or covering fire as a distraction.

The proper technique is to advance close to the wall, with the weapon in the ready position, and rotate only the barrel and head, never the entire body at once.

If there are multiple players, the first peeks and covers the front, the second aims at the left sector, and the third covers the rear.

Everything must be done in sync: if one stops, the others adjust their angles accordingly.

Another critical concept when dealing with corners is "slicing the pie." This technique involves gradually opening the field of vision in a semicircle, as if you were "slicing a pie."

Instead of rounding the corner abruptly, the player takes very small lateral steps, revealing the angle inch by inch and always keeping the replica aligned with their line of sight.

This minimizes risk and maximizes control over the angle.

It's a slow technique, but very safe, and is especially useful in spaces where snipers or enemies hiding in hard-to-see corners are suspected.

Priority management also applies inside rooms when entering from a hallway.

If multiple threats are present upon entry, the player must shoot first at the one who is armed and facing them, not necessarily the closest.

An enemy crouched behind a table with no line of sight can wait; one standing and aiming at the door must be taken out immediately.

In fast room clearing, the active threat takes priority over position, and line of fire is more important than distance.

6.3

Use of Flashlights and CQB Equipment.

The use of flashlights and CQB gear, such as grenades, flashbangs, smoke bombs, and specialized tools, is a crucial tactical component that can shift the balance in close-quarters environments, especially in urban combat scenarios, buildings, tunnels, or low-light interiors.

This equipment doesn't just add realism, it allows players to dominate spaces, break through defenses, disorient the enemy, and gain critical seconds during entries, room clearing, or extractions.

However, its use must be strategic, precise, and well-trained, as improper deployment can cause confusion among teammates or be wasted without any effect.

Tactical flashlights are key tools in dark or poorly lit environments.

They are mounted on replicas (preferably on lateral or bottom rails to avoid obstructing the line of fire), though they are also used on helmets or strapped to the wrist.

Their utility goes beyond simply "seeing better": in CQB, a powerful flashlight can momentarily blind the enemy, prevent accurate aiming, and force a retreat.

In nighttime scenarios, a sudden beam of light can create panic and facilitate a rapid entry, but prolonged or poorly managed use will easily give away your position.

Therefore, it's recommended to use flashlights with a momentary pressure switch (press to turn on, release to turn off) instead of leaving them on continuously.

The experienced player illuminates for fractions of a second, detects, shoots, and turns the light off.

For example, when entering a dark hallway, the flashlight is turned on for a moment to scan the layout of the room, then turned off, and the player advances with the replica already aimed at the most likely angle of threat.

Indirect lighting can also be used (pointing the light at the floor or wall) to avoid blinding oneself or directly alerting enemies.

BB grenades are devices that disperse pellets upon activation.

The most common types use spring, gas, or CO_2 mechanisms and come in various forms (pineapple-style, cylinders, 360° capsules).

They are effective for eliminating players inside rooms, around corners, or hiding behind structures.

Their use is simple in theory: throw, detonate, enter.

But in practice, timing and rebound direction are critical.

A poorly thrown grenade may fail to detonate or may land in a corner where its BBs don't reach the enemies.

That's why they must be thrown with technique: aiming for a bounce toward the center of the room or letting it roll under furniture to cover low areas.

In CQB matches with realistic rules, it's often enough for the grenade to go off inside the room for enemies to be considered eliminated, regardless of whether they were directly hit, this reinforces its tactical power.

Flashbangs (sound and light grenades) are replicas of stun grenades.

In airsoft, flashbangs don't produce a blinding flash like in real life, but they do generate a loud noise (some exceed 120 dB) or a surprise effect that can disorient the enemy.

In more realistic matches, their detonation can simulate disorientation for several seconds, and many trained players respect that rule: they crouch, don't fire, or remain immobilized for 5 seconds if they're inside the affected room.

A good flashbang is thrown just before entry, with a synchronized countdown: "Flash… one, two, go."

The player throwing it should briefly cover their ears and eyes if they are too close.

They should also train to throw it safely, avoiding rebounds that could send it back toward their own team.

Smoke grenades are both psychological and tactical weapons.

They are used to block enemy visibility, cover movements, enable extractions, or create confusion during an assault.

In CQB, they're used to obscure doorways, windows, long hallways, or exterior zones just before an entry.

A team that throws smoke at a building entrance can force the enemy to fall back or abandon their firing positions.

Properly used smoke creates a curtain of movement, players can advance through it in a zigzag, change direction without being seen, or even exit a building under pressure without taking direct fire.

However, smoke also affects those who deploy it.

If you haven't trained with it, it can cause disorientation, reduce internal visibility, or even enable an ambush from within the cloud.

That's why smoke should be deployed when you know what's on the other side, not as a blind improvisation.

There are also remote detonation devices or traps such as claymores, BB mines, or sound alarms.

These are placed on staircases, entrances, or choke points.

If the enemy doesn't detect them, triggering them can eliminate one or more players, or at the very least, alert the defending team of an infiltration.

Their use is more common in long matches or defensive missions.

A classic example: placing a tripwire mine in a hallway leading to a key room.

If the wire is triggered, a BB spray or sound charge is automatically released, alerting to the enemy's presence and blocking their advance.

As for additional CQB gear, highlights include tactical shields (sometimes made of reinforced plexiglass), replica-mounted cameras for clearing corners without direct exposure, holographic sights with red dots, laser aiming systems (used only in nighttime or indoor matches and with great caution due to eye safety), and hands-free communication systems.

In confined environments, response speed is significantly enhanced by proper equipment.

A player with a flashlight and shield can lead the entry, while another with a pistol clears tight spaces.

An operator with grenades can clear a room before anyone

enters, and one with smoke can cover an entire retreat without firing a single shot.

A common mistake among beginners is bringing all this equipment without training how to use it.

Poorly aimed flashlights blind teammates.

Badly thrown grenades bounce back and eliminate you.

Smoke bombs thrown without communication end up covering the enemy more than your own team.

In contrast, a CQB-trained team that practices entries, signals, grenade use, and light and smoke cover can take entire buildings in seconds, with efficiency and no casualties.

6.4

Coordination in Pairs and Trios.

Unlike open field environments, where space allows for wide maneuvers, in urban or indoor settings the close proximity between teammates and enemies demands movement as a fluid, compact, and reactive unit.

In CQB, pairs and trios aren't just practical groupings, they're the fundamental tactical structure for clearing rooms, controlling hallways, covering angles, and surviving in close-quarters combat conditions, where a half-second mistake can mean instant elimination.

A pair (two players) operates as a tactical cell that moves, covers, and acts in synchronization.

One of the two takes the lead (usually the more experienced or the one in front) and makes decisions regarding movement, entry, or fire.

The second player is responsible for covering the opposite sector, watching the rear, monitoring side doors or blind angles while the first player takes action.

During entries, player 1 goes in and clears the right side, player 2 the left, and both rotate automatically without needing to speak.

The coordination is so tight that each must understand what the other will do with just a gesture, a pause, or a tap on the shoulder.

In a hallway, the pair advances along the wall, one behind the other, with about 50 to 100 cm of separation.

The first player aims forward, while the second covers the sides and rear.

If there's a door on the right, the first player stops beside it, and the second passes and covers it.

Then they switch positions and decide whether to open, flank, or cover without entering.

When they enter a room, they divide the sectors: one turns right, the other turns left, never crossing paths.

Both advance two or three steps into the room, keep their replicas raised, make a quick scan, and give the "clear" signal with a word or gesture.

They never stay in the doorway or shoot from it, as it is the most exposed zone in all of CQB.

The trio (three players) adds another layer of complexity and versatility.

It allows for more complete entries, coverage of intermediate sectors, and an extra layer of security.

The third player can act as support, cover upper or alternative angles, maintain communication with the rest of the squad, or take the central position when the first two turn.

For example, in a classic entry, player 1 enters and moves right, player 2 goes left, and player 3 covers the center, aiming forward in case of an enemy deep inside the room or guarding a second door.

If the room has multiple entry points, the third player can secure one of the doors or throw in a grenade before the other two breach.

In well-trained trios, each player has a defined but flexible role.

If the first player goes down or is eliminated, the second automatically assumes the point role, and the third takes over the sector previously covered by the second.

These types of transitions are trained to become reflexes, there's no time to decide.

If a shot is heard during entry and one player is hit, the other two must push in, return fire, and secure the position without freezing from fear or hesitation.

The same applies if the trio is caught off guard in a hallway or hit by a grenade: they split up, one returns fire, the second retreats, and the third covers the exit.

Communication is essential and must be clear, brief, and unambiguous.

There's no room for yelling "over there, over there!, commands should be "right clear," "hallway one," "door closed," "covering," "entering."

Gestures are also used: open hand for stop, two fingers to the eyes for "watch," closed fist for "ready," index pointing down to mark a target or entry.

Many trios develop their own code systems for faster communication.

In low-visibility or high-noise scenarios, tactile signals are even used: one tap on the shoulder to move, two to stop, a long press to signal entry.

The movement formation of a trio can vary depending on the environment.

In a hallway, a linear formation is typically used: one player at the front, two covering the sides or rear.

In rooms, they form a triangle, with two players in front and one behind, mirroring each other's movements.

When advancing down a street with multiple building entrances, the center player can act as the anchor while the other two clear alternating entry points.

This flexibility allows the trio to advance quickly but safely, gaining ground without losing control.

In terms of weaponry, a CQB pair or trio usually uses short replicas, such as submachine guns or carbines with shortened barrels.

One may carry a shotgun or pistol for extremely tight spaces.

In more organized teams, one of the three might carry a flashbang or smoke grenade, and another a mounted flashlight or corner camera to inspect before entering.

They can also rotate roles depending on fatigue: after three consecutive entries, the lead rotates out and another takes point.

In CQB combat, there is no room for spacing errors.

In pairs and trios, every misjudged centimeter can result in crossing into a teammate's line of fire, tripping, or blocking forward movement.

That's why they train to move as a single entity, not as three individuals.

Each player adjusts their pace to match the others, avoids stopping abruptly, and knows how to fall back in an orderly way.

In a building clearance, this type of tactical unit can take room after room without the need for a full squad.

If they face a disorganized group, they outmatch them through coordination, fire discipline, and absolute synchronization.

6.5

Speed, Surprise, and Precision.

These three qualities cannot be separated or applied
individually, they function as a tactical unit: one enters
quickly, catches the enemy by surprise, and eliminates
with accurate shots.

If any of the three is missing, the operation breaks down.

In environments like buildings, houses, hallways, or
warehouses, where distances are reduced to just a few
meters and encounters are immediate, these qualities make
the difference between clearing a room without casualties
or being eliminated before even raising your weapon.

Speed in CQB is not about running recklessly; it's the ability to
enter a room, cover the assigned sector, and move to the next
point before the enemy can react.

Each player must know exactly what to do from the moment
they cross the doorway: which direction to turn, how many
steps to take, which sector to cover, and where to position
themselves afterward.

That speed must be trained until it becomes automatic.

If a player hesitates, stops abruptly, or looks to their
teammate unsure of where to go, it creates a bottleneck
and blocks the entry of the rest of the team, usually
resulting in elimination.

For example, when entering a hallway with three doors, a
well-trained pair can clear it in seconds: one covers forward,
the other turns and clears, and they move as a unit without
losing pace.

They don't run, but they don't stop to think either.

In CQB, slowness kills.

The goal is to take the room, secure it, and move on before the enemy has time to regroup or counterattack.

Surprise is the most powerful weapon in close-quarters environments.

A well-positioned enemy can be eliminated without ever firing a shot—if they aren't expecting your arrival.

That's why CQB assaults are built on disrupting the enemy's rhythm: entering where they don't expect, using a flashbang, banging on one door and entering through another, throwing a smoke grenade and going in through a window, faking a retreat and returning from the flank.

Surprise is created through silence, through the approach route, through nonverbal signals.

A classic example: a team simulates a frontal breach with noise, shouting, or light fire, while a trio flanks and enters through a side door completely unnoticed.

The first shot makes all the difference.

In CQB, there are no warnings, you enter, shoot, and dominate before the enemy understands what's happening.

Even one second of hesitation can be enough to take control of an entire room.

Precision is where many players fail, because in CQB there's no time to aim calmly.

A poorly placed shot can hit a teammate, miss entirely, or give the enemy time to react.

That's why shots are taken with well-configured replicas, equipped with fast-acquisition sights and absolute trigger control.

Here, the volume of fire doesn't matter, it's about the ability to land one or two quick shots on a visible target without losing control of the weapon or awareness of the environment.

Firing long bursts in a small room can be counterproductive, especially if teammates are inside.

The ideal method is double tap: two quick shots to the torso or head, followed by an immediate scan for the next target.

In realistic matches, players are trained to shoot only when they have total certainty of the target.

Accuracy is practiced in hallways, with moving targets or reaction drills using flashlights.

Entering blind and shooting on reflex often leads to friendly fire or unnecessary exposure.

The balance between these three qualities is what allows a team to clear a building without losing half its members.

If you're fast but imprecise, you enter first but miss the shot; if you're precise but slow, you take one out but get hit by the second; and if you're surprising but don't react decisively, you lose the element of surprise.

A well-trained CQB team knows exactly how to coordinate these three qualities.

For example: before entering, they throw a flashbang (surprise), breach as a trio in under two seconds (speed), fire controlled shots at visible targets (precision), and within five seconds, the room is secured.

Teams also train the ability to switch between modes in seconds.

A team may move quickly down a hallway, but upon reaching an intersection, they stop abruptly, assess the situation, throw a flashbang, and enter with surgical precision.

This alternation between rapid movement and fire control is achieved through constant training, repeating entry patterns, role rotations, and nonverbal coordination.

Even mistakes are part of the training: what happens if a replica jams? If a teammate goes down? If there are unexpected enemies in the room?

Everything must have an immediate response based on practice, not improvisation.

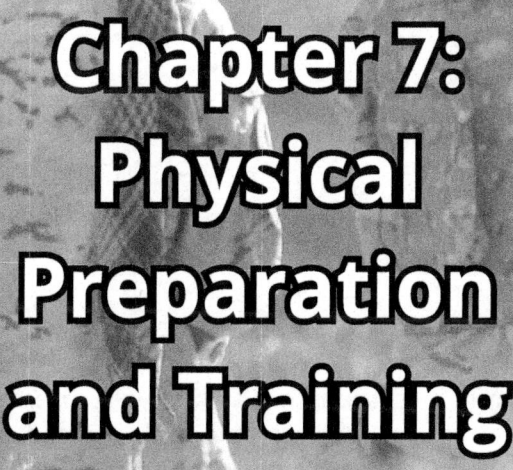

Chapter 7: Physical Preparation and Training

7.1

General Physical Conditioning.

It's much more important than many players realize.

Although this sport combines tactical simulation with strategy and roleplay, the truth is that physical performance can be the deciding factor between lasting through an intense full-day event or dropping out due to fatigue, cramps, injuries, or simply lack of mobility.

A well-conditioned player doesn't just run faster, they move with more control, crouch effortlessly, react more quickly, aim better under pressure, and recover faster between engagements.

Physical conditioning in airsoft is the silent foundation that supports all tactical skills.

The first priority is cardiovascular endurance.

In long matches, especially in open fields, milsim, or forest and mountain scenarios, players may walk, jog, and run for hours while carrying full gear: replica, vest, magazines, water, protection, radio, grenades, and sometimes even a backpack.

This can add between 5 and 15 extra kilos that the body must constantly carry.

If a player doesn't have a solid aerobic base, they'll start gasping for air after the first sprint, their heart rate will spike, shooting accuracy will drop, and their vision will blur from exhaustion.

Endurance is developed through regular running, cycling, or hiking sessions, ideally while carrying weight.

A very useful exercise is running with a loaded backpack, alternating between light jogging and short sprints, simulating the calm and combat phases of real airsoft scenarios.

Next is functional strength.

A player needs to be able to lift their own body weight quickly, crouch and stand repeatedly, hold their replica steady for several minutes, and climb or overcome obstacles without getting injured.

This isn't about aesthetic muscle building, it's about real power.

It's trained with exercises like burpees, squats, push-ups, planks, and bodyweight workouts.

Training with sandbags or kettlebells is also beneficial, as they mimic handling irregular gear.

If a player needs to crawl 10 meters under wire, carry an injured teammate (in simulations), or hike up a hill with full gear, they won't be able to do it without a solid base of general strength.

Mobility and flexibility are another essential component.

In CQB matches, players must move through narrow hallways, duck under furniture, round corners, roll, twist, and shoot from awkward positions.

Muscle stiffness can lead to injuries in the lower back, knees, or ankles, so training should include dynamic stretching routines, yoga, or joint mobility exercises.

Airsoft does not forgive clumsy movement: if a player dives into cover and lands poorly, they risk injury.

If they can't rotate their hips quickly, they remain exposed.

Body fluidity translates to tactical survival.

Coordination and agility also play a huge role.

Airsoft isn't linear combat, you have to move between obstacles, navigate trenches, climb stairs, zigzag, and change direction in milliseconds.

Training with agility circuits, foot ladders, cones, and visual reaction drills helps prepare both body and mind to move precisely without losing balance or efficiency.

For example, during a flank maneuver, a player might need to cross a ditch, dodge a barricade, make a 90° turn, and fire accurately, all in a matter of seconds.

This is only possible with a body that responds instantly.

Core training (midsection: abs, lower back, obliques) is probably the most important and underrated element.

Every long replica is supported by the body, not just the arms.

A strong core allows for stable shooting, firm torso movement, balance in awkward positions, and the ability to bear gear weight for hours.

Planks, bird-dogs, hanging ab exercises, and medicine ball work strengthen the body's foundation.

If a player gets tired just from keeping their replica shouldered or loses balance when firing from a kneeling or crouched position, they need to work on their core.

Lastly, there's physical and mental recovery.

A well-conditioned player doesn't just perform in the first engagement, they recover quickly and are ready for the next.

This includes proper nutrition, hydration, adequate sleep, and active recovery practices like post-game stretching or cold baths.

The mind is also trained: staying calm with an elevated heart rate, making decisions under physical stress, and not giving in to muscle pain.

A trained player knows how to breathe, move, shoot, and make decisions, even with a shirt soaked in sweat and trembling legs.

7.2

Aiming and Reaction Drills.

Aiming and reaction drills are essential for developing the ability to hit a target quickly, accurately, and under pressure, especially in realistic situations where there's no time to aim calmly and no margin for error.

It's not enough to have a good replica or an expensive sight if the player hasn't trained their body and mind to react, raise the weapon, align the aim, and fire within fractions of a second.

Aiming in airsoft is not just a technical skill, it's a tactical ability that must be trained just like movement or communication, and it must adapt to each environment, distance, and type of engagement.

The first critical aspect is fast and stable shouldering: many players aim well once the replica is already shouldered, but they fail when they have to raise it and shoot while moving.

That's why one of the most effective drills involves starting from a low-ready position (replica at the waist or pointed at the ground), receiving a visual or auditory signal, and raising the weapon with control, aligning the aiming elements (sights, red dot, or even iron sights), and firing a short burst.

This can be trained with static targets at short range—anywhere from 5 to 15 meters—and then progressed to moving or timed targets.

The key is to repeat the drill until the movement becomes automatic, without excessive tension in the shoulders or neck, and so that the first BB is accurately placed without needing mid-shot correction.

Another classic drill is the controlled double tap: two quick consecutive shots at the same target, aiming for both to hit a small area, such as the center of a silhouette.

This trains not only accuracy but also trigger control, sight recovery after the first shot, and replica handling under the pressure of a potential immediate engagement.

If the player's two shots are too spread out, it's a sign they need to work on their grip, breathing, or initial alignment.

Aiming while moving is one of the most useful skills in real matches.

Shooting while walking, during lateral or diagonal movements, or even when emerging from cover requires much greater coordination.

This is where the "shoot on the move" drill comes in: the player walks at a slow to medium pace toward a target, keeping the weapon steady, breathing with control, and firing at intervals.

At first, it may seem inaccurate, but with practice, the body learns to absorb the step recoil, keep the torso stable, and place effective shots even without standing still.

This is especially useful for CQB, where shots are rarely taken from static positions.

Reaction to unexpected contact is another critical training block.

This involves placing targets at hidden angles, behind corners, or using teammates who briefly appear with protection to simulate real contact scenarios.

The player must react with minimal delay, raise their replica, and fire with precision, without needing to empty the magazine.

Here, the focus is on speed with control.

A timer or random signal can also be used to force the reaction.

For example, the player waits with their replica lowered, hears a beep or a voice, and must turn, identify, and fire in under two seconds.

With a stopwatch and visible target, you can measure how many hits were made and where on the target, allowing for assessment of both reaction time and accuracy under pressure.

Target transition is also a crucial skill to practice, as in real combat, there is rarely only one enemy.

Knowing how to aim at one, fire accurately, shift to the next target, and shoot again without losing rhythm is critical.

This is trained by placing three or more targets spaced apart, simulating one, two, or all of them being threats.

The player must learn to "break" focus after each shot and move fluidly between targets.

This also improves peripheral awareness and decision-making: choosing which target to eliminate first based on proximity, position, or angle of fire.

Training with a secondary replica is also part of a complete routine, especially in CQB scenarios or situations where the main weapon runs out of ammo or malfunctions.

A fast transition to a pistol can save the match.

The typical drill involves firing with the primary weapon until a simulated malfunction occurs (or the magazine runs empty), letting it hang, and drawing the secondary to continue firing.

This movement must be completed in under 2 seconds and with full safety: without aiming at the ground, without dropping the primary, and without drawing the pistol with an open mouth or eyes off the target.

For advanced players, training also includes aiming under stress.

This is done with an elevated heart rate: running 50 meters, doing 20 burpees or squats, and then shooting immediately.

It simulates real combat conditions, where the heart is racing, breathing is irregular, and adrenaline affects stability.

Shooting while calm is not the same as shooting while sweating and breathless.

The player who trains under stress learns to control their body and accuracy even in adverse conditions.

Serious players also track their training: how many shots hit, how long they take, and what error patterns repeat.

This helps refine focus: if most shots go left, it might be due to excessive tension in the support hand.

If it takes too long to align the red dot, the sight height may need adjusting.

If the second shot misses, they may need to work on post-shot control,because every error has a cause, and every refined drill reduces a future risk in real matches.

7.3

Timed Drills.

Timed drills are one of the most effective tools for improving real-world performance under pressure, because they introduce time as an invisible enemy.

It's not just about shooting well, but doing it fast, accurately, and in the least amount of seconds possible, simulating real situations where a delayed reaction or slow entry can mean immediate elimination.

The stopwatch turns a basic drill into a mental and physical challenge: it creates stress, forces quick decisions, and reveals weaknesses that would go unnoticed at a slower pace.

One of the fundamental exercises is reactive shooting with a start beep.

The player starts with the replica in a low-ready position, not aiming.

At the sound of the timer or shot clock (which can be a sport shooting app), they must raise the weapon, aim at the target, and fire one or two shots.

The time stops when the target is hit.

This drill measures reaction speed, aiming setup, and the ability to shoot without hesitation.

It's repeated multiple times, recording the times to track improvement.

For example, if in the first sessions it takes 2.5 seconds from the beep to the impact, with consistent practice that can be reduced to 1.7 seconds or less.

Another popular drill is "El Presidente," adapted from dynamic shooting: the player starts with their back to three targets placed in a line, and at the sound of the timer, they turn, aim, and fire two shots at each target, for a total of six shots.

Time is measured from the beep to the final hit.

This drill demands coordination, target transition accuracy, shooting control, and situational awareness.

In airsoft, it can be done at 5 to 7 meters with torso targets or smaller silhouettes, and it's ideal for comparing performance between players or tracking weekly progress.

In CQB, the timed room-clearing drill is commonly used.

Three to five targets are set up inside a room or structure (cardboard cutouts, silhouettes, pop-up targets), and an entry point is designated.

The player must enter, identify targets, shoot, and exit, all while the clock is running.

This type of practice trains not only reaction speed, but also visual scanning, target prioritization, and accuracy in confined spaces.

A player who enters chaotically, aims at everything without a logical sequence, or fails to control their line of fire will lose valuable seconds.

The goal is to enter, hit all targets, and exit cleanly in the shortest time possible.

Timed Fire + Reload Drills are also part of training.

The player fires a set number of BBs (for example, five), performs a simulated reload (drops the magazine, inserts a new one, hits the bolt catch if the replica includes it), and continues firing.

The timer runs from the first shot to the last.

This measures response time to an unexpected reload, something common in real situations.

Difficulty can be increased: running 10 meters beforehand, doing it from a kneeling position, or from behind cover.

Timed movement drills are also essential.

The player must move from point A to point B, stopping at two or more shooting stations.

For example: start from cover, run 5 meters to a cone, shoot a target; advance another 7 meters to cover, shoot another; and finish at a third position firing from a crouch.

Each segment can be timed, or the entire course timed as one.

This simulates real combat movement, where precision is needed despite fatigue and elevated heart rate.

A useful variation is mirror training: two players perform the same drill separately, under the timer, and compare results.

This not only adds pressure but also introduces a friendly competitive element.

The player who can maintain speed and accuracy while mentally competing against another improves at a much faster rate.

You can also perform a physical circuit + timed shooting drill.

For example: do 15 burpees, then pick up your replica and shoot at three targets, or run with a backpack, drop to the ground, crawl three meters, get up, and fire at a target.

Here, the timer measures endurance, recovery under fatigue, and the ability to shoot with stability after exertion.

This type of drill is ideal for simulating a player's real condition in an intense match, where shots are not taken from a comfortable position, but after continuous physical effort.

You can even train with a mental timer, without shooting: practice shouldering the weapon, acquiring the sight, controlling breathing, and "simulating" the shot while timing the entire process.

This sharpens reflexes, streamlines movement, and builds awareness of how long your body actually takes to perform a technical action.

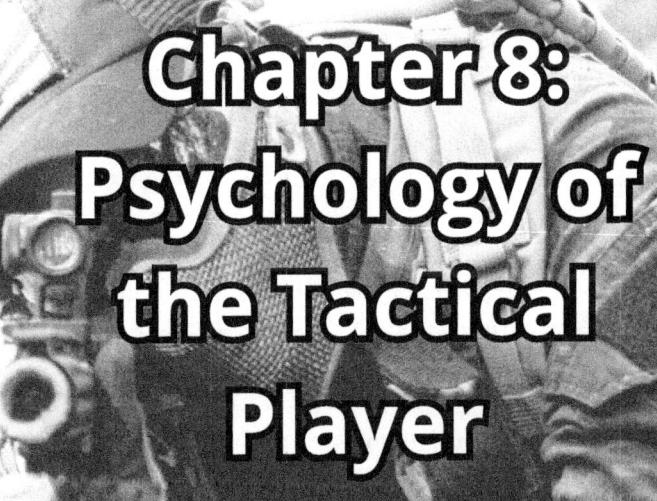

Chapter 8: Psychology of the Tactical Player

8.1

Stress Control, Adrenaline, and Focus Under Fire.

This is one of the most decisive aspects of real performance on the field, especially in intense situations such as CQB combat, ambushes, sudden flanking, or prolonged milsim games.

Although airsoft doesn't involve real physical danger, the brain reacts physiologically as if it did: heart rate spikes, hands shake, vision narrows, muscles tense, and thoughts become clouded.

A player who hasn't trained their response to stress tends to shoot erratically, make poor decisions, panic, or freeze, right when clarity is needed most.

Stress in simulated combat arises the moment a player feels at a disadvantage, realizes they've been spotted, or needs to move while under fire.

On a physical level, the sympathetic nervous system is activated: heart rate increases, breathing becomes shallow, fine motor skills decrease, and vision narrows into a "tunnel," cutting off peripheral awareness.

This leads to rash reactions, firing without aiming properly, shouting unnecessarily, forgetting to reload, running in a straight line, or losing contact with teammates.

That's why learning to manage this adrenaline surge is essential for any serious player.

The first tool to control it is tactical breathing, a simple technique that allows you to regain focus within seconds.

It involves inhaling deeply through the nose for 4 seconds, holding for another 4, exhaling through the mouth for 4 seconds, and repeating.

This box breathing calms the nervous system and reestablishes the connection between mind and body.

It can be applied right before entering a room, while under fire, or after a sprint.

A player trained to breathe this way during combat reduces shaking, sharpens aim, and acts more logically.

In simulations, many teams train to take a breathing pause before an assault, even if it's just 3 seconds.

Another key technique is anchoring attention to the present, meaning avoiding thoughts like "I'm going to get eliminated," "I'm alone," or "we lost the round."

The player must focus solely on their next immediate action: "cover the door," "move to the wall," "throw the grenade."

That kind of focus reduces mental paralysis.

A player who gets distracted by future thoughts or self-doubt stops hearing their squad, forgets their assigned sectors, and becomes a liability.

Trained operators repeat internal mantras like "advance calmly," "breathe, aim, shoot," or "control my zone" to stay centered.

Adrenaline management is trained through intense and progressive scenarios.

A new player suddenly thrown into a CQB with shots coming from all directions will likely freeze.

But if they first train with slow simulations, then with sound, then with a timer, and finally with real contact, their body adapts.

For example, doing drills with loud music or random beeps while shooting forces the brain to make decisions under pressure.

Training immediately after running, when the heart rate is elevated, does the same.

This simulates the effect of an ambush or prolonged firefight.

A common mistake is to get carried away by excess adrenaline.

Some players enter what's known as berserker mode: they run, shout, and shoot uncontrollably.

Although it may seem effective, they usually end up overexposed, run out of ammo quickly, and lose situational awareness.

Control doesn't mean slowness, it means acting fast with a cool head.

The best player isn't the one who shoots the fastest, but the one who, even while being hunted, keeps breathing, changes cover efficiently, and shoots with surgical precision.

In milsim or long-duration matches, sustained focus is another major challenge.

After hours in the field, under heat, cold, or hunger, the mind begins to drift.

It becomes easy to stop watching a flank, miss a signal, or lose contact with the squad.

This is where mental endurance, self-motivation, and internal protocols come into play.

Some players establish mental "check-in" routines: every 10 minutes they review their sector, ammo, team position, and extraction point.

It's also helpful to rotate roles or positions to keep the mind alert.

Even in a static defense, a player can slip into a relaxed state and fail to hear an approaching enemy if they haven't trained their awareness.

The best way to train concentration under pressure is through realistic drills with clear consequences.

For example, if a player fails to watch their sector and allows the enemy to flank, the entire squad must retreat or restart.

That kind of "tactical penalty" teaches players not to make the same mistake.

Stress shooting is also part of training: a contact signal is given, the player is forced to advance under simulated fire (e.g., shots against a shield or near them), and then given a clear order, to shoot three targets in a specific order.

Only those who keep a cool head will succeed.

8.2

Rapid Decision-Making.

It's not just about knowing what to do, but deciding it within seconds when the environment shifts, teammates go down, enemy fire erupts from an unexpected angle, or the initial plan breaks apart.

A player who hesitates, freezes, or needs to confirm every step during an active situation will be taken out, or worse, compromise the entire squad.

In contrast, the one who makes fast decisions with tactical logic, emotional control, and terrain awareness turns uncertainty into an advantage.

The key to deciding quickly is not impulsive improvisation, but having trained internal criteria that allow you to act automatically based on the situation.

For example, in CQB, if a player rounds a corner and sees two enemies, one crouched nearby, the other farther away but aiming directly at them, there's no time to think.

If they've trained threat prioritization, they'll know to eliminate the one with the line of fire first, even if he's farther away.

That decision, made in under a second, is based on learned and confidently applied rules of engagement.

Another classic example: a squad comes under flanking fire while advancing down a hallway.

The leader must decide in under three seconds whether to fall back, take cover and return fire, or throw a distraction grenade and keep pushing forward.

If you wait for everyone's opinion, chaos follows.

Here, decision-making is based on three factors: available information, knowledge of the team, and tactical urgency.

If you know there's cover 5 meters ahead and the enemy has no crossfire, you can decide to push forward.

If, on the other hand, the fire is intense and there's no cover, the immediate order should be: "Back! Take cover! One covers, two falls back!"

In many matches, players use the mental technique of the "rule of threes": if you spot a threat, quickly think of three things — Does it see me? Does it have an angle? Can I move without getting exposed? — and act based on that.

This trains rapid analysis.

In drills, players are forced to make quick decisions: for example, they're presented with a fork and a contact signal, and must choose right or left without discussion.

Whoever decides quickly and maintains initiative breaks the balance of the engagement.

Decision-making is also trained through controlled failure.

If a building entry plan fails due to more enemies than expected, the team must adapt: retreat, switch entry point, use a grenade, or create a distraction?

At that moment, waiting for outside instructions can be fatal.

That's why pairs are trained to have "Plan B" protocols that activate if they don't receive orders within 3 seconds.

A duo that enters and encounters resistance might decide to flank the building from the right while deploying a smoke screen, without being told to do so.

That kind of tactical autonomy improves with experience, but also through scenarios where intelligent initiative is rewarded.

Another key factor is risk management.

A well-trained player knows when to take risks and when not to.

For example, if they're defending an objective and end up alone, they can choose between staying hidden or moving to eliminate approaching enemies.

The decision must weigh: How many are left? How much time remains? Is it better to surprise or hold?

An impulsive player runs and shoots without thinking.

A hesitant one stays still until they're eliminated.

A mentally trained player makes the most logical decision under pressure.

In night games or large terrain, decision-making under limited information also comes into play.

You can't see the enemy, you only hear gunfire.

This is where patterns are applied: if the sound is coming from a lower area, it's likely a flank; if it's short bursts, it might be suppressive or diversion fire.

The player must decide whether to hold position, alert the team, or quietly reposition.

There's no time to ask for validation.

Squad leaders also have to make decisions for everyone,

and the hardest part is doing it without having all the information.

Sometimes, you have to split the squad, send one group to flank, another to create a distraction, knowing it might fail.

But waiting to "see what the enemy does" almost always ends in defeat.

The player who makes quick decisions, even if imperfect, keeps the team moving and retains the initiative.

And in airsoft, as in any simulated combat, initiative matters more than volume of fire.

One useful technique is role-playing in drills: putting each player in the leader's position and giving them a situation with just 5 seconds to decide.

"Your teammate is down, you've lost comms, and you hear gunfire 10 meters away… what do you do?"

This practice trains fast thinking under pressure and allows players to correct impulsive or hesitant decisions.

It also teaches them to live with mistakes, making quick decisions means sometimes getting it wrong, but not deciding at all is worse.

8.3

Emotional Leadership, Team Spirit, and Motivation.

This is not an individual game, it's a tactical and collective experience where success depends not only on who shoots, but on how the group stays united under pressure, how morale is managed when everything goes wrong, and how leadership is exercised with both the head and the heart.

A player who knows the map but not their squad is incomplete.

A leader who gives orders without connecting with the team will fail.

And an operator who doesn't know how to lift their teammates after an ambush isn't useful in the most demanding matches.

Emotional leadership in airsoft means more than just giving commands.

It means understanding that each player reacts differently to stress, defeat, or frustration.

An emotionally intelligent leader can recognize when someone is panicking, when someone else needs a boost, when to stay silent, when to listen, and when to push.

During a milsim game, for example, a player may start to show signs of fatigue or frustration after several hours without progress.

The leader could push harder and burn them out… or switch their role, assign them a lighter task (like lookout, relay, or support), and make them feel they're still a valuable asset.

That not only preserves tactical cohesion, it also boosts the morale of the entire team.

Team spirit is built before the first shot is fired.

It's cultivated during training, in downtime, in the jokes before the match, and in how roles and responsibilities are shared.

A strong team doesn't need to be physically together all the time, it's mentally connected.

They know each other by movement, cover one another without being asked, and support each other unconditionally.

During a CQB assault, if one player goes down, the other doesn't hesitate to recover their replica, pull them back, or cover their retreat under fire.

Not because someone ordered it, but because the team has built a bond where each member is worth more than their kill count.

That kind of cohesion makes the group function as a unit, not as scattered pieces.

Positive and emotional leadership also shines in the most intense moments.

When an operation goes wrong, when the enemy takes the upper hand, when multiple positions are lost or key players are out, the leader who stays calm, gives clear direction, and emotionally reconnects the team to the objective is the one who prevents the squad from falling apart.

Sometimes, all it takes is a phrase like, "We're taking this back," "Switch to the flank, regroup, we've got this," or even, "It's okay, this is part of the game."

Words like that, said with confidence, stabilize morale and refocus the team.

Silence, on the other hand, fills the space with fear and doubt.

Motivation in airsoft is a mix of adrenaline, camaraderie, and purpose.

But it's not always running high.

In long games, with fatigue, heat, rain, or tactical confusion, morale can drop quickly.

A good team knows how to lift it: small victories are celebrated, the player who took a risk is acknowledged, and the one who held their position well, even without firing a shot, is valued.

Motivation can even happen mid-combat: "Nice shot!", "Great cover, brother!", "Let's go, we're breaching now!"

These phrases, when said with authenticity, fuel the team's emotional engine.

The strongest teams also know how to use tactical motivation.

They don't just say "we have to win", they give clear reasons to move, like "if we take that hill, we'll have full visibility," or "if we secure that house, we control the enemy spawn."

A player motivated by a concrete goal fights harder, even when exhausted.

And a leader who turns each maneuver into a reachable objective creates momentum even when the team hesitates.

Another dimension of emotional leadership is managing egos.

In mixed teams, with both new and veteran players, tensions can arise.

The emotionally capable leader gives everyone a voice, allows each player to shine in what they do best, and corrects without humiliating.

A mistake becomes a lesson: "Next time, wait for the signal," not "You screwed up."

A success becomes reinforcement: "That flank was perfect," not just "Nice shot."

That kind of communication strengthens the team from within.

There's also silent leadership, the kind that doesn't need words but inspires through action: the one who enters first without fear, who stays behind to cover, who shares their water, replica, or magazine without hesitation.

In airsoft, this kind of leader earns respect without formal rank.

Their presence motivates more than any shouted command.

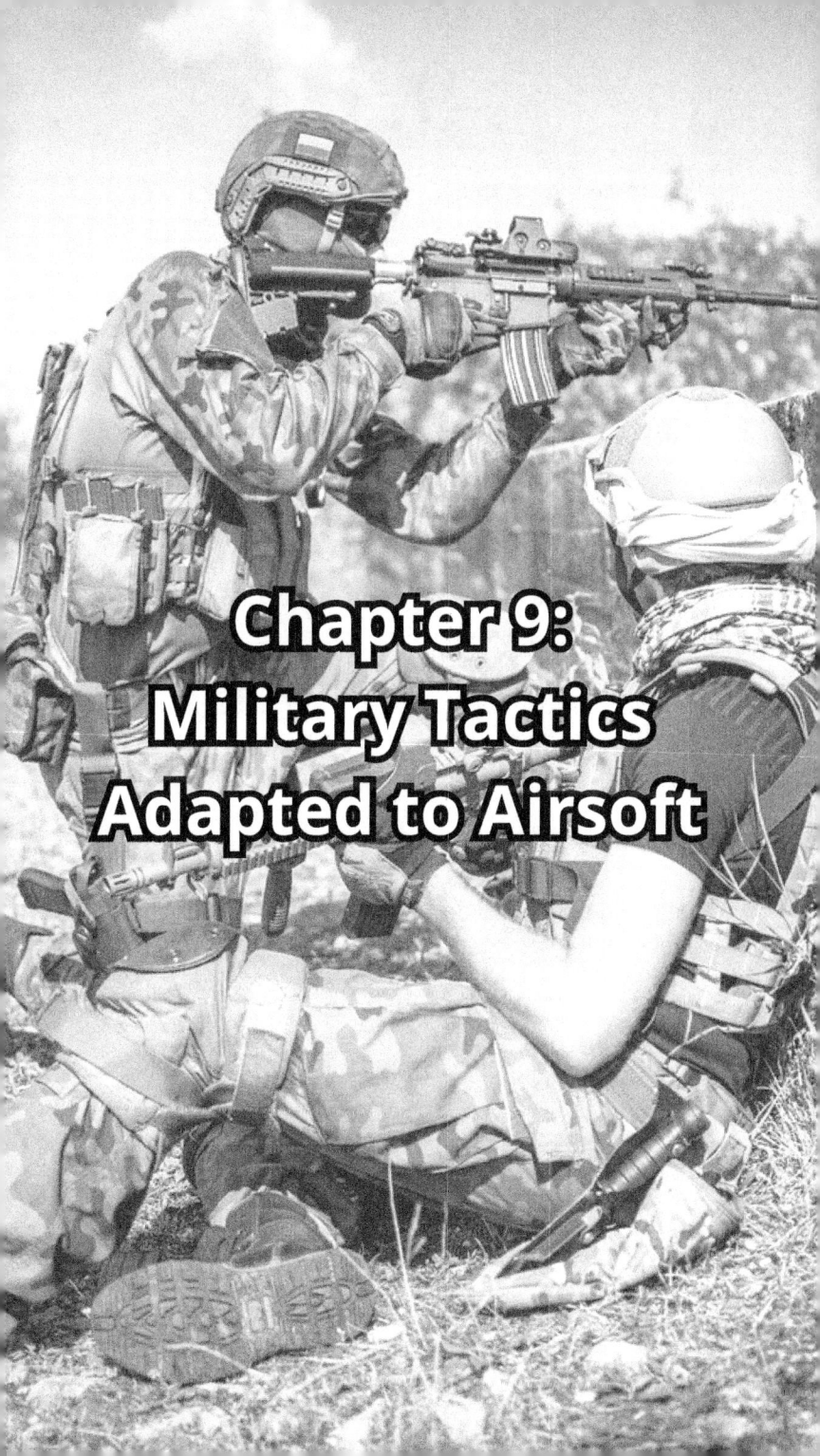

Chapter 9:
Military Tactics
Adapted to Airsoft

9.1

What We Can Learn from Real Infantry.

Although airsoft is a sport and not warfare, infantry military doctrines have been successfully adapted by many players and squads, as they allow for greater tactical efficiency, group cohesion, and operational effectiveness.

What sets an advanced player apart from a beginner is not their replica or camouflage, but their ability to think and move like a real soldier: anticipating, covering, communicating, reacting, and fulfilling their role within a team.

One of the first lessons we can learn from infantry is the use of sectors and shared responsibilities.

In a real squad, each soldier has an assigned field of vision, a designated fire sector, and a clear role: one covers the front, another the right flank, another the rear.

There are no redundancies or blind spots.

In airsoft, many eliminations happen because two players are aiming at the same spot while the enemy appears from another.

Applying this principle means every player must know their role and not break formation without reason.

Even in a small trio, the field of fire is divided into 120 degrees per operator, ensuring full coverage.

Another key infantry principle is fire and movement.

Real soldiers don't all charge forward at once, nor do they all stay back and shoot.

They alternate: while one covers, another advances; while two are firing, the fourth moves to the next piece of cover.

This translates perfectly to airsoft: a duo in a hallway can alternate between firing and zigzag movement; a squad can flank while a pair maintains frontal pressure.

This technique keeps continuous pressure on the enemy without exposing the whole team.

It's trained until it becomes automatic, there's no need to say "advance," it's enough for one to start firing and the other knows it's their turn to move.

We also learn the importance of cover and terrain usage.

Real infantry is trained to move from cover to cover, never cross open areas without supporting fire, and always advance with the lowest profile possible.

In airsoft, this means hugging walls, using vegetation, shooting from low or elevated positions, and never staying in the same spot once detected.

A player who uses the terrain like an infantryman, rolling, crawling, using angles, and moving silently, becomes an extremely difficult opponent to detect or eliminate.

Decentralized leadership is another legacy of infantry that applies directly to airsoft: when a military squad loses its commander, the next in line takes control.

There's no total dependence on a single figure.

In complex matches, this doctrine translates to each squad being able to operate autonomously, completing objectives without waiting for new orders.

Even within a unit, if the leader goes down, another player

must know the plan and continue the operation.

This means everyone must be familiar with the map, objectives, fallback routes, and comms codes.

Radio discipline and silent signals also come directly from infantry tactics.

In real operations, no one yells "over here!" or "he's in the window!"

Clear, concise, and calm terms are used instead.

In airsoft, adopting phrases like "contact right, 30 meters, flank covered" or "moving 5, cover me" improves communication, reduces confusion, and prevents the enemy from overhearing.

In addition, the use of hand signals—raised fist for stop, two fingers for eyes, open palm for advance—allows for silent operation, which makes a huge difference in CQB or infiltration scenarios.

Another fundamental concept is situational awareness.

An infantry soldier learns to read the terrain, anticipate movements, understand the enemy's intent, and stay alert even when there's no visual contact.

In airsoft, many players drop their guard when they don't hear gunfire, and that's exactly when they get ambushed.

Learning to move with constant awareness, checking flanks, observing footprints, listening for environmental changes, and anticipating enemy routes transforms the entire gameplay experience.

A player with an infantry mindset doesn't just react, they anticipate.

From the infantry, we also learn physical and mental endurance.

A soldier is trained to operate while tired, cold, hot, or fatigued, without losing effectiveness.

In milsim or long-duration games, the player who has trained for that endurance has the advantage: they keep covering their sector, keep communicating, keep fulfilling their role when others are already exhausted.

In night games, under rain, or after hours of marching, a player with an infantry mindset maintains composure, discipline, and motivation.

That inner strength is trained just like marksmanship, by progressively exposing oneself to demanding scenarios and learning to manage body and mind.

Even casualty handling and tactical retreat is a direct lesson.

A soldier doesn't stay behind out of pride.

If the position is unsustainable, they retreat in order, deploy smoke, recover the wounded, or fall back to the next defensive line.

In airsoft, this prevents unnecessary eliminations, preserves resources, and allows for fast regrouping.

The team that knows when to hold and when to retreat tactically is the one that strikes back hard minutes later.

And finally, the infantry teaches us the most important value of all: operational unity over individualism.

A soldier doesn't fight for their personal score, they fight for their squad, their mission, and their teammate.

In airsoft, the best teams are those where gear is shared, teammates cover each other, and they give praise and correction without ego.

Where no one leaves behind an eliminated teammate, and everyone understands that success doesn't depend on a "lone hero," but on a well-organized formation, a coordinated advance, and a strategic retreat when needed.

9.2

Techniques from Units like SWAT, SEALs, SAS and Their Practical Application to the Game Field.

In airsoft, applying techniques from real-world units like SWAT, the Navy SEALs, or the British SAS not only raises the level of play but completely transforms how a squad operates.

These elite units have developed protocols, movements, and tactics tested in real combat environments, tactics that can be perfectly adapted to the field to maximize efficiency, coordination, speed, and effectiveness.

While replicas shoot BBs instead of bullets, the logic behind every movement—cover, angles, synchronization, room clearing, entry, and terrain control—is nearly identical in a high-level tactical game.

1. SWAT (Special Weapons and Tactics):

Over decades, they have developed a set of tactics specifically designed for combat in tight urban environments, where every second and every corner can be lethal.

These techniques aren't just used in hostage situations, barricades, or extreme threats, they can be applied very effectively to airsoft, especially in CQB (Close Quarters Battle) settings such as buildings, abandoned factories, hangars, or urban fields designed for simulation.

One of the most well-known and effective techniques is the stack formation for tactical entry, where operators line up one behind the other beside a door.

The first in line, also known as the "breacher" or "point man," is responsible for initiating the entry into the room.

They may carry a shotgun, a simulated battering ram,
or simply be the first to clear the area.

The second and third follow immediately, each covering a
specific zone upon entry: right, left, front, ceiling, or floor.

The fourth covers possible secondary exits or threats from
stairways.

In airsoft, this technique is replicated exactly the same way
and is essential for maintaining speed and space dominance,
the key to any effective room clearing.

Right before entry, the "slice the pie" technique is used—
also known as "cutting the pie" or "slicing the corner"—which
involves gradually peeking around a door or corner without
exposing the whole body.

The operator slowly rotates around the angle, clearing
sections of the room from the outside, identifying potential
threats, and improving visual coverage without full exposure.

In airsoft, this is extremely useful for detecting traps,
static enemies, or players waiting in blind spots.

Another vital SWAT technique used in airsoft is the
simultaneous dynamic entry from multiple access points.

If a room has two doors, the team splits into two cells that
breach at the same time through both entrances.

This "collapses" the room from within, breaks the enemy's
firing line, and maximizes confusion.

In airsoft, this technique is highly effective when coordinated
by radio or visual signals.

For example, one team throws a flashbang through one door while the other breaches from the opposite side.

The psychological impact and spatial dominance created are immense.

Another common tactic is the "buttonhook entry," where the first two operators entering the room both turn to the same side (instead of splitting left and right).

It's used when the enemy is suspected to be entrenched in a single sector or when the shape of the room justifies it.

It's especially useful in small rooms or those with obstacles.

In airsoft, it allows players to control a specific angle without spreading forces too thin.

The use of flashbangs (stun grenades) is also a standard SWAT tactic and is widely used in airsoft CQB games with a certain level of simulation.

In scenarios where sound or light devices are permitted (including models that emit flashes and loud noise without being pyrotechnic), tossing a flashbang before entry disorients the enemy for several seconds.

In airsoft, this is typically enforced with rules like: "if it explodes in the room and you're inside, you're disabled for 5 seconds."

This tactic gives the attacking team a major advantage, if timed perfectly.

Another essential concept is 360-degree control once the room has been secured.

Instead of staying fixed or lowering their guard, players must immediately cover interior doors, stairwells, windows, or ceilings, since threats can come from any of these points.

A player who has just entered and cleared their corner can rotate to cover another zone.

This constant rotation of fire sectors is a hallmark of the SWAT style and, in airsoft, allows players to hold positions without becoming vulnerable to counterattacks.

Tactical hierarchy without shouting is another important lesson.

During an entry, there's no time for long commands.

Body language, a shoulder tap, a hand signal, or a single keyword ("breach," "cover," "moving") is enough.

In airsoft, training with these signals prevents chaos during combat and enables the team to enter, clear, and advance without even speaking in full sentences.

SWAT teams also train with ballistic shields at the front, this technique can be replicated in airsoft using polycarbonate tactical shields.

A player with a shield advances, absorbs incoming fire, and allows their partner to shoot from behind with cover.

This is especially useful in tight hallways, tunnel entrances, or open areas with little natural cover.

The shield can be rotated to protect a flank or absorb a burst while the team repositions.

Airsoft can also incorporate techniques like "check left–check right", where every time a player crosses a doorway or turns down a hallway, the first operator does a quick scan to both sides before stepping forward, while their teammate covers blind angles.

This technique prevents ambushes in L-shaped corridors or buildings with multiple branches.

One of the most important takeaways from the SWAT approach is the idea of "rapid action with total control": it's not about rushing in blindly, but entering quickly, with every operator knowing exactly what to cover, how to move, and when to rotate.

In airsoft, when a team applies this, they can take entire buildings, clear house by house, secure upper floors, and eliminate enemies with no more than five shots exchanged.

The difference lies in prior training, disciplined movement, and clarity of roles, not in the volume of fire.

2. Navy SEALs:

The elite special operations force of the U.S. Navy, Navy SEALs are renowned for their ability to operate autonomously, in small units, and in highly complex hostile environments.

In airsoft, SEAL techniques translate directly to milsim games, night scenarios, infiltration missions, long-range patrols, or high-precision objectives.

What defines their style isn't just their gear or appearance, but their mindset: meticulous planning, silent execution, and absolute resolution of objectives, without relying on excessive firepower.

A central technique in their doctrine is silent movement through hostile terrain, which translates perfectly to airsoft when advancing through forests, abandoned structures, or areas with multiple natural covers.

SEALs don't walk in a straight line like a traditional platoon, they use formations such as inverted V, staggered line, dispersed column, or compact diamond, depending on the terrain.

In airsoft, this means players don't bunch up like a row of targets, they spread out their profile, maintain tactical spacing (2 to 5 meters), and constantly turn their heads to maintain 360° awareness while moving.

Each player knows which zone to monitor and moves with soft steps, avoiding dragging their replica, not hitting branches or rocks, and maintaining visual contact or using frequent hand signals.

Non-verbal signals completely replace voice communication.

A closed fist means "stop," a hand extended downward means "crouch," two fingers pointing to the eyes followed by a gesture toward a location means "visual contact," and a hand on the back followed by pressure means "fall back."

In airsoft, using this system reduces the chance of detection and improves the fluidity of movement.

Even in games without radios, a team fluent in hand signals can coordinate like a real operational unit.

Upon reaching an intersection or fork, the leader raises a fist, the rest crouch, a silent scan is made, and the advance is decided with a single gesture.

Another key principle is: "two is one, one is none", meaning every duo must operate autonomously.

If one player is taken out, the other must be able to continue the mission without relying on outside support.

In airsoft, this translates to forming solid pairs where both operators know the objective, the map, radio codes, escape routes, and safe zones.

If one is eliminated, the other isn't left without a plan.

Each pair should carry duplicate materials: grenades, map, radios, med kit, IR light if playing at night.

In a long match, a player who relies entirely on their partner for every action will lose effectiveness at the first unexpected event.

Simultaneous entry from multiple points is also a SEAL trademark.

Instead of entering through a single door, they split into assault cells that synchronize their entry through different access points of a building.

In airsoft, this tactic dismantles enemy defense by breaking their focus: if they expect a frontal breach but the attack comes from the flank and rear, there's no time to reorganize.

For example, one team throws a sound grenade through a window to distract, while another breaches through the back door in a tight formation.

In 10 seconds, an entire structure can be cleared before defenders have a chance to respond.

Advanced reconnaissance is also part of the SEAL playbook.

Before any attack, a detailed observation of the target is conducted: number of entrances, building height, areas with cover, possible escape routes, estimated number of enemies, and patrol patterns.

In airsoft, this can be applied even without drones or high-tech tools: it's enough to send a recon pair that gets within 30 meters without being seen, memorizes positions, and returns to the main team with visual or sketched intel.

That information allows the team to plan the attack with total advantage, avoid traps, and choose the ideal moment to breach.

SEALs also train for surgical interventions in hostile zones, such as hostage rescues or eliminating a specific target without collateral damage.

In airsoft, this can translate to missions where a figure (VIP player or symbolic item) must be extracted from a well-defended building.

The technique includes silent infiltration, use of smoke or light for distraction, sector-based coverage, and fast extraction to a secure point.

A team that masters these techniques can win without having to eliminate the entire enemy squad, they just need to execute with precision, coordination, and speed.

Another highly effective SEAL tactic for long matches is rotating field leadership.

Instead of centralizing command, decision-making roles are distributed: if the main leader is cut off, another steps up and continues the mission.

In airsoft, this means that each squad or pair has a sub-leader capable of executing orders without waiting for full instructions, and everyone knows the mission objectives.

This speeds up gameplay, reduces downtime, and keeps pressure on the enemy without hesitation.

Additionally, SEALs follow the principle of minimal force, maximum effectiveness: they don't fire impulsively.

They fire only when it's safe, necessary, and precise.

In airsoft, this means not revealing your position unless absolutely necessary, conserving ammo, not shouting when scoring an elimination, avoiding blind fire, and relocating after each shot.

A SEAL-style operator in airsoft can take out three players silently, without anyone knowing where the shots came from, and move out before being detected.

Terrain usage as a tactical weapon is also essential: moving against the light, using shadows, sight lines, elevation, reflections, and environmental sounds (wind, water) to mask movement.

In nighttime or forest games, this makes a critical difference.

A player who knows how to move through vegetation, stop when hearing branches, hide behind rocks, or follow dry creek beds becomes virtually invisible.

3. The British SAS (Special Air Service):

The SAS has profoundly influenced many modern special operations doctrines, and their aggressive, autonomous, and adaptable style fits perfectly with the demands of high-level tactical airsoft, especially in milsim games, infiltration scenarios, night operations, or simulations with complex rules.

Their philosophy of "strike, destabilize, and disappear" translates powerfully to the field, enabling teams to dismantle the enemy without prolonged engagements, overexposure, or reliance on superior numbers.

One of the most representative techniques of the SAS is deep penetration with withdrawal under fire, which involves executing a surgical rapid incursion into a hostile zone— a base, camp, convoy, or fortified point—completing the planned action (such as eliminating a target, extracting a resource, placing a symbolic "charge," or gathering intel), and then immediately withdrawing under a structured cover: smoke to block enemy vision, crossfire to stop pursuit, predefined escape routes, and regrouping at a safe point.

In airsoft, this playstyle translates into squads that don't stay to defend the area they just captured, but instead understand that their advantage is the element of surprise, and once the objective is fulfilled, they vanish as if they were never there.

For example, a team can storm an occupied structure, plant a simulated mine or eliminate a key operator, throw a smoke grenade down the stairwell, and fall back, exchanging no more than 10 shots.

Another classic technique is Close Target Recce (CTR), which in airsoft terms means approaching high-risk zones —like an enemy spawn, control point, fortified base, or simulated antenna—without being detected, observing for several minutes, counting enemy forces, identifying routes, weak points, blind spots, and patrol routines, and returning to relay that information.

This requires absolute stealth, both visual and auditory camouflage, and terrain mastery.

In airsoft, a squad might perform a CTR during the first third of the match to determine when and where to strike later, using that intelligence advantage to plan an ambush or decisive assault.

A team that executes a solid CTR has already won half the match before firing a single shot.

The SAS is also known for the versatility of its operators.

Instead of fixed, rigid roles, each member is trained to perform all essential functions: accurate shooting, treating teammates, using radios, leading if needed, handling simulated explosives, navigating by map, and making tactical decisions.

In airsoft, this doctrine is applied by training every squad member to be self-sufficient.

If the leader goes down, the second-in-command takes over without hesitation.

If the medic is eliminated, another can perform the simulated treatment.

If communication with the team is lost, any member knows how to return to the rally point or follow plan B.

This ability to operate with or without visible leadership turns the team into a fully functional, independent unit.

The SAS also excels at using mobile ambushes.

They don't just wait in a fixed location, they position themselves at choke points (paths, valleys, bridges, narrow corridors), fire from multiple angles, create chaos for 20 to 30 seconds, and then relocate before the enemy can react.

In airsoft, this can be trained with pairs or trios that fire from concealment, release 10–15 well-placed BBs, and shift 10 meters to another firing point before the enemy can pinpoint them.

The psychological effect is devastating: the opposing team starts firing in all directions, while the real operators are already flanking from another angle.

Another SAS tactic that can be applied is the use of deliberate distraction.

For example, they simulate a frontal assault with controlled fire, flares, noise, or lights, while another team infiltrates from the rear or plants an objective.

This technique allows you to pin the enemy exactly where you

That balance between autonomy and tactical cohesion is what makes an SAS-inspired airsoft squad a formidable force.

want, forcing them to react to an apparent threat while the real one moves unchallenged.

In well-organized airsoft matches, a SAS-style team can simulate a retreat, provoke pursuit, and lead the enemy into a pre-set ambush.

They also stand out for their use of micro-attack patterns, which consist of relying not on one large offensive, but on small, constant, coordinated actions: eliminating a sentry, cutting off communication, stealing enemy resources, or capturing a side flag.

Each of these actions destabilizes the opponent.

In airsoft, this means not focusing only on direct combat, but on eroding the enemy's structure without overexposure.

Even their communication style is unique: they use brief codes, key words, and tactical silences.

In airsoft, applying this allows for radio communication without revealing anything useful (in case of eavesdropping) and without overloading the channels.

Phrases like "red contact," "moving echo," "clear angle," or "Alpha 2 secured" replace long-winded communications and ensure operational efficiency.

Finally, the SAS prioritizes the value of individual initiative within a team structure.

Each operator has the freedom to adapt to the terrain, change their route, or modify their approach if they see the original plan is no longer viable.

In airsoft, this means training players to think, decide, and act without needing permission, but always within the framework of the common objective.

Printed in Dunstable, United Kingdom